PRAISE FOR DR. JEAN

"If you have ever dreamed of taking a class from the highly regarded scholar Dr. Jeana Jorgensen, this comprehensive text will grant your wish. Dr. Jorgensen's presentation of material in *Folklore 101* is organized logically and supported with an array of significant sources and suggestions for further study. Her examples illustrate each concept beautifully, her writing prompts encourage critical thinking and reflection, and her friendly, laid-back narrative style makes learning about folklore studies fun. You'll want to *be* a folklorist after reading this book!" - Susan Redington Bobby, editor of *Fairy Tales Reimagined: Essays on New Retellings*

"Jorgensen welcomes readers into folklore studies with clarity and humor. Her straightforward explanations shape genres and theories into readily useable tools, while brief, engaging examples energize students to tackle their own analysis. By leading students to recognize the significance of the folklore all around us, Jorgensen makes a persuasive case that the study of folklore matters because 'it allows us to keep a finger on the pulse of what people *actually* care about.'" - Patricia Sawin, Associate Professor of Folklore and American Studies, University of North Carolina, Chapel Hill

"Jeana Jorgensen's research in Folklore, both the academic and the public-facing, rectifies common misperceptions, engages with popular fascinations, and persistently pushes the field forward into the 21st century; these are also the strengths of *Folklore 101*. Jorgensen engages historical scholarship while demonstrating the ongoing, immediate relevance--and wisdom--of the field through discussions of memes, urban legends, and more. It succinctly presents the concepts most crucial to the field of folkloristics in a manner that is both thorough and extremely readable--this is not just a book for scholars, but for anyone with an interest in folklore. In its entirety, it would be perfect for any Folklore classroom, and individual chapters are marvelously condensed overviews of complex topics that could be used in any classroom where folklore is discussed." - Psyche Ready, Independent Folklorist, English PhD student at University of Connecticut

CONTENTS

BASIC FOLKLORE CONCEPTS

BIG CATEGORIES OF FOLKLORE

FOLKLORE GENRES

SPECIAL TOPICS

DEDICATION

My mom likes to joke that I was born reading a book. I can say without a doubt that my entire family has been my biggest support system in encouraging my love of reading, writing, learning, and teaching, so thank you Mom, Dad, Sam, Grammie, Papa, Auntie M, and the rest of our extended family for always believing in me. This first book is for you!

And, of course, to my folklore mentor, Alan Dundes: this book is my interpretation of the way you made folklore come alive in the classroom.

INTRODUCTION: WHAT IS FOLKLORE AND WHY DOES IT MATTER?

Welcome to Folklore 101! This book is my version of a DIY folklore class, compiled from my teaching materials, essays, and blog posts over the years. It's meant to be accessible and fun, showcasing serious research concerns as well as funny examples while also proving that not all academic writing needs to be boring and dry. Since folklore is a huge topic, I can't cover every single aspect of it in this book, but I can give you a decent grounding in basic folklore scholarship, so you can go on to explore the folk groups and genres and topics that speak to you the most!

I'm a folklorist by trade: I've devoted my entire adult life to the study of folklore (and I was interested in it as a kid before I knew it was an official subject one could study), so obviously I think it's pretty important. Calling something folklore is a compliment in my book, a statement that it's worthy of serious study, which is a line I'm borrowing from my mentor Alan Dundes, who received death threats when he wrote about the Bible as folklore. I lucked into studying with Dundes at UC

Berkeley as an undergrad, before knowing that he helped establish the foundations of modern folklore studies and that, prior to his death in 2005, he published nearly 40 academic books and 250 scholarly articles.

Of course a folklorist saying, "Hey, that's folklore!" is the ultimate compliment, which is part of why Dundes perhaps wasn't expecting the death threats. Classifying something as folklore doesn't mean it has no truth value or that it's not meaningful to people (which is where I think the death threats stemmed from; critics were hearing "The Bible is just folklore, it's untrue" whereas Dundes was saying "The Bible shows many hallmarks of being passed down along through oral tradition before it was written down and standardized"). I open by mentioning this death threat drama because it exemplifies what it's like to be a folklorist: most of the time, it doesn't feel like people take folklore or folklorists very seriously, but when folklore does become a hot topic, oh boy, things might get tense!

I mean, I'm sitting here writing this introduction during a global pandemic, which has been fueled in part by urban legends (a folklore genre!) and conspiracy theories around vaccines and the efficacy of home remedies (hello, folk medicine) and which has also inspired lots of homemade arts and crafts, from sourdough baking (foodways!) to whole new levels of crafting (folk art). Folklore is the social glue that holds us together - or helps tear us apart - and boy is it showing right now. What people learn face-to-face, peer-to-peer, through oral tradition or internet tradition, is often aligned with what they value, and hence can fly under the radar of or conflict with official/institutional knowledge transmission. This is one of the reasons why it's often so tough for pro-vaccine and anti-vaccine people to have a conversation where they both hear each other (as my colleague Andrea Kitta has documented): they're each drawing on different knowledge registers from different types of sources, plus they're usually very emotionally invested in the topic. People being invested in beliefs rooted in communally-held values? That comes from our interactions with folklore over our life cycle, whether it's about deeply-held beliefs about gender presentation (do women have to shave their legs to be feminine?) or what counts as healthy food and healthy bodies (don't get me started on fatphobia in the U.S.!) or even what counts as a good story or joke. Every single thing related to values in a culture doesn't necessarily count as folklore, which I'll define here shortly, but I truly believe that if you want to understand a culture, you must look at its folklore, and that's what got me started on this journey in the first place.

Enough about me. Whatever brought you to this book – intellectual curiosity, your professor is making you read it, you're related to me hence obligated to buy it – I am hoping you'll find something intellectually and/or creatively stimulating here. You don't have to read the book in order, though if your teacher is telling you to, maybe consider following through on that. I've structured the book in four main sections: basic folklore concepts, big categories of folklore, folklore genres, and special topics. My bias towards verbal folklore and narrative genres is evident throughout, so if you're a fellow lover of stories and/or storyteller, you've definitely come to the right place!

To understand what folklore is, you need a basic sense of what culture is first (and here, I borrow heavily from my colleague Lynne McNeill's excellent book *Folklore Rules*). I'll give a few different definitions of folklore in this introduction, but right now my favorite is McNeill's "informally transmitted traditional culture."

So what is culture? Again, there are tons of definitions, but I go with McNeill: culture is learned and transmitted, and it's what you need to know to act normal in a society. Culture is the web of beliefs, behaviors, languages, arts, and so on that fleshes out a society, that gives it a life beyond "here's what's legal and here's what's illegal, good luck."

I want to focus on the fact that culture is learned: it may be inherited via family systems, but it is NOT inherited genetically. There's nothing in your genes that makes you predisposed to one cultural thing over another. I sometimes see biological deterministic language applied to culture (Dawkins and memetics, I'm looking at you) and I'm not a fan of that approach. There might be some useful overlap in natural phenomena and cultural phenomena worth exploring, but culture is distinct from nature precisely because it is transmissible outside of the natural sphere; culture can encourage people to contradict their instincts instead of giving in to them. You can change your culture by moving elsewhere and acclimating to a new one, but you can't change your genetic makeup (yet?). And so on.

Culture has many components to it, and according to my favorite definition, folklore is a part of culture. It's located within culture. But where a cultural anthropologist might specialize in any number of the different parts of culture like kinship or migration, a folklorist specializes in the portion of culture that is informally passed along and is traditional in nature.

Folklore refers to the parts of culture that are not institutionalized in the same way that the government or religion are (though folk religion is definitely a thing). "Informally transmitted" means that folklore is performed and passed on through means that exist outside the official sphere of...whatever. Laws, the education system, medicine, and so on. Those locations still have people saying and doing and making folklore, but it's not necessarily found in the HR handbook or the legal code: it's just people in their jobs having slang and stories and customary ways of doing things (more on this in the chapter on occupational folklore). We're especially likely to find folklore where people gather face-to-face and don't have the same kinds of weighty hierarchies as in institutions.

While there's been a lot of interesting scholarship on risk in folklore – like if you tell an off-color joke, what are you risking? What are the consequences for you in different contexts? – folklore is in some ways inherently less consequence-bound than official/institutional culture. Like, if you break the law while driving, you could be facing a ticket or fine or jail time. But if you tell a joke badly, or don't manage to pull off a traditional holiday dish...there might be social consequences? Maybe even rather nasty long-term ones? Those look pretty different than being tossed into the criminal justice system, though.

There are at least two other interesting things about folklore being informally transmitted. The first is that folklore can, as a result of this trait, take damn near any shape that humans can come up with. No one's gatekeeping it the same way that blockbuster movies require financial backing, advertising, a whole team to make it go and give it a chance of success. So if you're skimming the Genres section of this book and you're like "how are a fairy tale and Halloween and folk medicine all basically the same thing?!" it's because what makes these things folklore is not that they all look exactly the same superficially, it's because people transmit them informally rather than through institutional channels. The other neat thing is that tradition and variation (covered more in-depth in the next section) are hallmarks of folklore, meaning that – unlike with the law – there's no "official" version of any one kind of folklore. When a movie is filmed, or when a book is published, that product is the official version, barring a ten-year-anniversary release with added/updated material or something like that. But with folklore, your version of a knock-knock joke is as valid as mine, and while one of us might tell the joke with more artistry, or more incisive social commentary, neither one of them is necessarily truer or righter or better.

Nope, I lied, there are at least *three* interesting things about folklore being informally transmitted, and this last one I'll talk about here ties back into the purpose of this introduction: explaining why folklore matters. See, because folklore is passed along informally, it maintains relevance or it dies out. There aren't generally laws saying we need to keep traditions alive in highly specific ways; there isn't a folklore canon the same way there's a literary canon. If folklore doesn't meet people's conscious or unconscious needs somehow, there's no reason to transmit it, and it ceases to be. I go into this more in the chapter on functions, but this is, in a nutshell, why folklore matters: by tuning in to it, it allows us to keep a finger on the pulse of what people actually care about, whether or not they admit it to themselves. And that, in my mind, is very powerful indeed.

Okay, on to the other word in my preferred folklore definition: tradition. As in, folklore is informally transmitted traditional culture. As I mentioned above, tradition will get its own discussion, because it's that important. Briefly, tradition doesn't necessarily have to mean centuries-old stuff that's remained unchanged that whole time. Tradition refers to anything that is continuous or stable over time, and moreover, a stable-over-time thing that is shared to some degree (yes, there is a debate over personal/solo traditions; no, I'm not getting into it right now). If it's shared and it's stable enough to document popping up in multiple instances, that counts as tradition for our purposes. And indeed, this is why folklorists count memes and lolcats as traditional: their time on this planet may be very short indeed, but enough people are sharing them that they're definitely a thing.

One final thing, and this is something I think my favorite definition sadly lacks: truth value. Folklore has a neutral orientation towards truth value. Calling something "folklore" in the slang sense of the word might mean you're saying "oh, that's just folklore" or "oh, that's just a myth" or "oh, that's just a fairy tale" or "oh, that's just an urban legend" – all of which are used to mean "oh, that's fake." We don't use any of those terms in folklore studies to mean fake. As you'll see, each genre I just named has its own specific conventions and traits that, among other things, specifically help the audience go in with an assumption about that genre's truth value or lack thereof. When we call something "folklore" in this academic area of study, we are NOT saying anything about its truth value. That assessment is not built into the definition of folklore, like, at all. It is a definition that tells us about folklore's relationship to the rest of culture, indicating that folklore is more likely to be a bit more ever-shifting and variable than the mass media or the institutions of law, government, and medicine. I know that fairy tales as folklore are usually not true in any factual sense of the word (no one thinks "Once upon a time" leads into a true biographical story), though fairy tales may reveal emotional truths, or truths about a culture's core values. By the same token, I know that some folk medicine may be factually true: people were chewing on willow bark to help with pain before anyone figured out that the active ingredient, salicylic acid, could be turned into aspirin.

So please please please, mentally separate "folklore" and "true/untrue" in your mind. When we're categorizing something as folklore, we generally want to know more about the how of its transmission than the what of its contents, though that turns out to be important on the level of genre classifications later on, too.

If you've gotten this far in the introduction, congrats, you now have a working definition of folklore as informally transmitted traditional culture! I'm going to nerd out about folklore definitions a bit more here, so feel free to keep reading if you want to dig deeper, and then I'm going to end this chapter by debunking some falsehoods and assumptions about folklore and folklorists.

Two other short-ish definitions I like for folklore are "artistic communication in small groups" by Dan Ben-Amos and "creativity in everyday life" by Pravina Shukla. Hopefully these make a lot of sense given the discussion of the various ramifications of "informally transmitted" and "traditional culture" above, but what I like about these definitions is their special focus on art and creativity: we're not tuning into Art-with-a-capital-A as in the fine arts, the masterpieces created by (mostly) dead white dudes, or the classical music composed by more of the same. Those things are great and all, but they're not the same cultural data jackpot that folklore is. Folklorists care about what people do in their daily lives that connects them to a tradition, past, and/or community that is larger than they are. We look for the balance point between the individual and the group, between the mundane and the transcendent. Sometimes folklore can feel mundane since it's not always surrounded by neon blinking lights saying "Important Art/Culture Stuff Happening Here!!!" But small acts of daily connection can also be incredibly meaningful: shared rituals like prayers at the dinner table or like using the blanket knitted or quilted by a relative can imbue simple things with emotions and memories. And we think these things are worth paying attention to.

That last paragraph was all very affirming, but we also hit some complications when we look at other definitions of folklore. The term "oral tradition" has been used synonymously with "folklore" for a while now; back in the 1800s, "popular antiquities" was another recurring phrase to describe the same type of stuff (though it also has some problematic assumptions baked in, such as the notion that folklore is inherently super old, which is not always true). As Alan Dundes, among others, has pointed out, saying that folklore = oral tradition can be misunderstood when you're looking at a culture that's nonliterate or doesn't rely as heavily on literacy to transmit knowledge. Does that mean every single piece of information they pass on using the spoken word is folklore? Of course not. There are also some genres of folklore that aren't transmitted in the spoken word at all; some genres exist entirely in writing, such as latrinalia and yearbook verses and chain letters, while others aren't transmitted in language so much as in bodily behavior (like body art and folk medicine).

Because of all these difficulties, Alan Dundes famously pivoted away from the folklore = oral tradition definition, instead asserting that if you break "folklore" down into "folk" and "lore," you get folk groups (with its own chapter below!) which are groups that have any single identifying factor in common. A folk group could be as large as a nation, ethnicity, or religion, or as small as a family, hobby group, or set of classmates. These folk groups would then have traditions they call their own, shared beliefs and knowledge and behaviors and stories that reinforce their sense of identity with one another. That's the "lore" side of things.

Of course, this could all come across as still too abstract to wrap one's head around, and that's why Dundes decided to provide an itemized list of folklore genres to give beginners something to latch on to. I'm replicating that list here in case it's helpful for y'all.

> Folklore includes myths, legends, folktales, jokes, proverbs, riddles, chants, charms, blessings, curses, oaths, insults, retorts, taunts, teases, toasts, tongue-twisters, and greeting and leave-taking formulas (e.g., See you later, alligator). It also includes folk costume, folk dance, folk drama (and mime), folk art, folk belief (or superstition), folk medicine, folk instrumental music (e.g., fiddle tunes), folksongs (e.g., lullabies, ballads), folk speech (e.g., slang), folk similes (e.g., blind as a bat), folk metaphors (e.g., to paint the town red), and names (e.g., nicknames and place names). Folk poetry ranges from oral epics to autograph-book verse, epitaphs, latrinalia (writings on the walls of public bathrooms), limericks, ball-bouncing rhymes, jump-rope rhymes, finger and toe rhymes, dandling rhymes (to bounce children on the knee), counting-out rhymes (to determine who will be "it" in games), and nursery rhymes. The list of folklore forms also contains games; gestures; symbols; prayers (e.g., graces); practical jokes; folk etymologies; food recipes; quilt and embroidery designs; house, barn, and fence types; street vendor's cries; and even the

> traditional conventional sounds used to summon animals or to give them commands. There are such minor forms as mnemonic devices (e.g., the name order Roy G. Biv to remember the colors of the spectrum in order), envelope sealers (e.g., SWAK—Sealed With A Kiss), and the traditional comments made after body emissions (e.g., after burps or sneezes). There are such major forms as festivals and special day (or holiday) customs (e.g., Christmas, Halloween, and birthday). (Dundes 3)

No need to memorize that list, thank goodness, but hopefully you can see how everything named would also count as informally transmitted traditional culture rather than something handed down through the literary canon or law or med school. It's not an exhaustive list, either; memes didn't exist when Dundes was writing it in the 1960s, though xerox-lore in office settings at that time might provide a close parallel.

Finally, I'll clear up some misunderstandings that exist about folklore and folklorists:

- "Folklore" can refer both to the subject matter and to the field of study, so often you'll see us distinguishing between the two by calling the subject matter "folklore" and the field of study either "folklore studies" or "folkloristics" (modeled after how the study of language is called linguistics)
- "Folklore" as a word does not get pluralized; it doesn't make sense to write or say "folklores." If you really need to indicate that something is plural, go with

"folklore items" or "folklore texts." It also works better as a noun than an adjective; I would just append "folk" in front of nouns that I want to indicate are folkloric in nature, so I'd be more likely to say, "I'm analyzing folk stories" than "I'm analyzing folklore stories."

- Folklorists don't always perform the genres we study. I am terrible at telling jokes, and yet I study jokes. However, there are plenty of examples of scholars who get so immersed in their fieldwork that they do end up picking up a musical instrument in the folk music tradition they're studying, or perhaps their personal interest in a given genre is what got them started studying folklore.
- Folklore encompasses more than fairy tales and urban legends; I happen to be one of the folklorists who primarily studies fairy tales, but you can't assume every one of us can give a lecture on the Grimms at the drop of a hat.
- Most folklorists don't write children's books or worship everything written by Joseph Campbell and we get cranky when you suggest these things to us (many of us don't have the time or inclination to write popular fiction, and Joseph Campbell has misrepresented and cherry-picked examples of folklore in ways that annoy us).

Hopefully this introduction has given you everything you need to understand what folklore is and why it matters. Remember, folklore is transmitted voluntarily, because it is relevant to people's personal and social lives in some way, even if that way is not immediately obvious. By tuning in to folklore, you're tuning in to what actually matters to people, the kinds of culture they are choosing to keep alive by participating in it.

References:

Dundes, Alan. "What Is Folklore?" In *The Study of Folklore.* Prentice Hall, 1965. 1-3.

McNeill, Lynne S. *Folklore Rules: A Fun, Quick, and Useful Introduction to the Field of Academic Folklore Studies*. Utah State University Press, 2013.

BASIC FOLKLORE CONCEPTS

TRADITION & VARIATION

I FORESHADOWED this pretty heavily in the introduction: understanding tradition and variation is key to understanding what folklore is and how to study it. Heck, "tradition" is included in most definitions of folklore, including my current preferred definition: folklore is informally transmitted traditional culture. In this chapter, I'll go deeper into what tradition is and what its counterpart variation is, as well as giving you some tools to observe these dynamics in the world around you.

(Not gonna lie, I kinda just want to tell you to read the "Variation and Tradition" section of chapter 1 of Lynne McNeill's excellent book *Folklore Rules* but noooo, I had to go and decide to write my own book on folklore, I brought this on myself so now I have to do the work! But I will quote heavily from McNeill, so enjoy the fangirling!)

With tradition, there tends to be a misconception that the only things that count as "traditional" have to be, like, centuries old, super quaint, and definitely in the realm of antiques. Folklorist Barre Toelken, instead of using tradition and variation in his scholarship, wrote about conservatism and dynamism, and I think that switching over to conservatism for a second here helps demonstrate the sense in which we're actually using tradition: something has to be stable, continuous, and have a thread of sameness about it. It doesn't have to be millennia old or etched in stone to count as traditional, it just has to show some sort of continuity over time and space. You have to be able to identify a thread connecting past to present, whether that past was ten days ago or ten years ago or ten centuries ago.

As with so many facets of folklore, it really does make sense as a cohesive whole. This is what McNeill has to say about it:

> Remember, identifying folklore is all about identifying how it travels; if it hasn't traveled at all, then it's simply not folklore. In fact, if it hasn't been shared, it's simply not 'folk' – remember, 'folk' implies 'culture,' which implies 'group,' not a single person. That's why we so often call folklore 'traditional'–it gets passed on from person to person, leaving multiple versions in its wake. (12)

How much do I love this quote? If it were shorter, I'd consider getting it tattooed on me somewhere. I love that it highlights the manner in which folklore is transmitted, essentially peer-to-peer if not face-to-face, and the ways in which it becomes tied up in group identity. Folklore is what people do in groups when they're hanging out, regardless of whether they're thinking of it explicitly in those terms (I pretty much never hear groups of people being like "We're gonna go do some Folklore now" unless they're going to listen to the new Taylor Swift album of that title).

I also love that the McNeill excerpt focuses on how folklore travels, leaving multiple versions in its wake. McNeill and I both studied under Alan Dundes, and he was famous for (among other things) his criterion for figuring out whether some fascinating new thing you just encountered is folklore or not. The phrase he used is "multiple existence and variation," which is a slightly different riff on "tradition and variation," as I'll explain, using a real-world example, after talking about variation some.

I do want to note that tradition, while folklorists are super drawn to it, is not inherently a force for good. Some customs that are traditional harm people, and some scholarly conceptions of tradition can be used to keep marginalized people stuck on the margins. As my colleague Rachel González-Martin notes: "Tradition is a racialized tool. The academic concept of tradition is an organizational device that undervalues racialized communities in our contemporary Western, White society, where Whiteness is synonymous with 'unmarked' and tradition is part of a validation of a community's capacity to historicize its existence in place and time" (36). In other words, when white/USAmerican (to use González-Martin's term) scholars wield the term "tradition" it can almost be a way of putting other groups down, saying "oh, isn't that quaint and charming." But González-Martin also identifies why tradition is so powerful: "Tradition is a set of practices that hold both literal and symbolic values" (36). When we tune in to what a society deems traditional, we're seeing what the people in that society have decided to delineate, with a big neon arrow, as these things hold value to us. And that is pretty darn useful to us as students of culture.

Next, we tackle variation (or as Barre Toelken calls it, dynamism). Variation can occur at any level of folklore: in the phrasing if it's a verbal genre, in the plot if it's a narrative genre, switching out characters for one another in narrative genres, and so on. Basically, variation means that things aren't set in stone when folklore is on the table, which is quite different from when you're discussing other realms of culture. McNeill writes about this too, but you might imagine folkloric variation as being like a game of telephone, where the "original" message warps into bizarre variants by the time it makes its way around the circle. However, in folklore, there is no original, or if there once was, it's been lost to the sands of time, so it's practically useless to even think in those terms, unless you have a time machine I guess.

In contrast, other modes of culture have really different relationships to variation. Elite culture in the Western world – fancy things for upper-class people – might include stuff like operas, ballets, and classical music, where those creative texts stay essentially the same but are reinterpreted anew by performers. There's not supposed to be a lot of variation except in the artistic execution, and straying from the source texts without warning is frowned upon. The audience, incidentally, is also a small sector of society: rich, upper-class people, and those that have been married or socialized into those ranks. Pop culture and mass media, on the other hand, are intended for pretty much everyone: newspapers, TV shows, movies, novels, graphic novels, and so on. Their intended audience is quite wide, but their level of variation is still on the small side. Once you've printed a newspaper, the articles might be reprinted but there's no reason to change up the phrasing unless a correction needs to be issued. Once a film is cut and released, it will be shown exactly the same way in every movie theater and on every streaming service (unless a special director's cut edition comes out too). The gatekeeping is similarly high in elite culture and mass culture: small numbers of (ostensibly talented) people produce and perform the texts for consumption.

Cultural material travels between these modes, too. Certain ballet and theater texts are based on folklore ("King Lear" is based on a near-incestuous "Cinderella" variant), while folklore sometimes parodies the fine arts. Fanfiction is a giant arena in its own right, with pop culture characters being narrated in highly democratized, folkloric ways. Many fairy tales started in the realm of folklore and oral tradition only to be snapped up by Disney and brought into the realm of pop culture as films, toys, costumes, and storybook spin-offs. But while you can't really copyright folklore because it always exists in multiple versions, Disney has done, er, interesting things with copyright law, and as a result, certain fairy-tale images are off the table for anyone not employed by them.

The arrival of the internet, of course, has changed some of this. Where you used to need big money and a crew to make a movie, now you can film something on a smartphone and broadcast it on YouTube. Anyone can host a podcast these days. So the types of gatekeeping in production and transmission have definitely shifted. Still, it remains a pretty drastic difference between intentionally making a podcast or YouTube video – of which only one version exists at a time, unless you are constantly going back and re-editing your stuff, ugh, why – and telling a joke that is retold in slightly different ways every time and is 100% accessible to anyone who speaks that language.

Thus, folklore is inherently democratic in ways that other forms of culture just...aren't. This doesn't mean that folklore is inherently good, though. As the chapters on jokes and legends reveal, folklore isn't just rainbows and unicorns, it's also dead babies and nasty stereotypes and slut shaming. So, just like my little rant in the introduction about how labeling something folklore doesn't have any bearing on its truth value or lack thereof, here's a mini rant about how labeling something folklore does mean that it's democratically transmitted, as in, it's accessible to most anyone in that folk group, but we can't get sucked into a democratic = good association. Sometimes folklore promotes stereotypes that should die in a fire, which is one reason I discarded the idea of using a joke in this chapter to illustrate variation, because the joke managed to be both transphobic and misogynist but it also kinda critiques misogyny depending on the version you're working with (multiple existence and variation at work!) and...I decided it wasn't worth it.

So, the go-to example for this chapter, to show tradition and variation as well as the related concept of multiple existence and variation, is going to be Biden memes instead. Really, though, you could find any highly formulaic joke – knock-knock jokes or "Why did the chicken cross the road?" – and see what I'm talking about, that folklore simultaneously stays the same and is different or made anew in each telling.

Memes exemplify folklore well for a variety of reasons, though they may not be the first thing people think of when they think of folklore. First, the "tradition" element of memes is not very old, which can throw people off if their mental definition of folklore includes the tag of "quaint old stuff" (again, totally unnecessary to define folklore that way). Additionally, it's not uncommon for people to think of technology and folklore as being diametrically opposed to one another; where one flourishes, the other doesn't yet exist, or perhaps is defeated. This, too, is overly simplistic. While evolving technology may directly impact folk technologies such as spinning, weaving, knitting, and quilting, leading those forms of folklore to shapeshift or become more specialized or rare, folklore is always more about the informal nature of its transmission than about the involvement of technology in its landscape.

Memes, or image macros, count as folklore because they are informally transmitted traditional culture. Anyone with a device connected to the internet can make and transmit them, hence fulfilling the "informally transmitted" part of the folklore definition. And what makes them traditional is that they build upon one another, upon shared understandings of the world, drawing together both internet and face-to-face ways that people communicate and make meaning. Other types of folklore also thrive on the internet, such as chain letters (which existed in the analog world prior to the digital world), superstitions, and storytelling. My colleagues engaged in the study of internet folklore analyze everything from Slender Man to anti-vaccine online groups to sick humor around sports scandals (check out my colleague Trevor Blank for this last one in particular).

Take a category of memes, and one can demonstrate the existence of both tradition and variation. The same picture of Morpheus from the film *The Matrix* has become the traditional backdrop for a meme starting with the words "What if I told you…" and then the remainder of the phrase is what varies, providing endless riffs on whatever the maker wishes to comment on in the meme.

Further, using the idea of multiple existence and variation backs up the interpretation of memes as being folklore. Many memes come in cycles, or groupings of similar topics or social commentaries on the same event. If I came across a single meme using an image that no one else had ever used before, that commented on a topic that no other meme was about, I am seeing the existence of a singular text, not multiple existence. I'd probably assume that meme was someone's attempt to start a trend, and it didn't resonate with other people, so it didn't take off. One of the main ways of thinking about tradition, as noted above in McNeill's work, is that it's shared and passed on, between and among groups. If there's no passed-on-ness to an item on the internet, it's probably not of interest to folklorists.

So if you ever encounter something you think is cool, and you're wondering if it's folklore, aim to document multiple existence and variation. Can you find more than one example of the thing? And then, do the examples show some differences among them? When I lecture on fairy tales, one of the classic examples is a beloved tale like "Cinderella" or "Little Red Riding Hood": there are hundreds or more versions of these tales circulating (multiple existence), and they often have tons of little differences from one another, like where in the Grimms' "Cinderella" she's given magic dresses to go to the ball by the birds who live in the tree growing from her mother's grave, whereas in Perrault's "Cinderella" the fairy godmother gives her everything (variation).

The last time I actively decided to document some folklore for research purposes, I played the "multiple existence + variation" game in my head with the Biden memes that arose during the 2016 U.S. presidential election. Days after the election, I noticed the memes popping up on Twitter and Facebook, showing (former) Vice President Biden booby-trapping the White House in true *Home Alone* style in order to make incoming President Trump's stay short and miserable. I immediately verified multiple existence and variation because there were dozens and then hundreds of these memes (multiple existence), and they all tackled different facets of Biden's tricksy plans (variation). They were all clearly showing more or less the same thing, Biden playing tricks on Trump (tradition), while riffing on lots of different potential scenarios, from Biden changing the TV language to Spanish to Biden putting shrimp shells in the curtain rods (variation).

As I collected these memes, having established through multiple existence and variation that they weren't just an isolated phenomenon of little interest to folklorists, I also began to look for common themes and potential meanings and functions. I gave a few lectures on the subject, to my college students and to colleagues, in order to feel out my interpretations. I teamed up with my friend Linda Lee to coauthor a book chapter on the topic, where we advanced the rather specific hypothesis that Biden acts as a boundary-crossing trickster in these memes to relay not only humor but also political discontent. It was a fun project to work on...and it was possible because, from the very beginning, I was attuned to tradition and variation.

References:

González-Martin, Rachel. "White Traditioning and Bruja Epistemologies: Rebuilding the House of USAmerican Folklore Studies." *Theorizing Folklore from the Margins: Critical and Ethical Approaches*, edited by Solimar Otero and Mentz Auanda Martínez-Rivera, Indiana University Press, 2021, 22-41.

Jorgensen, Jeana, and Linda J. Lee. "Trickster Remakes This White House: Booby Traps and Bawdy / Body Humor in Post-Election Prankster Biden Memes." *Folklore and Social Media*, edited by Andrew Peck and Trevor Blank, Utah State University Press, 2020, 129-144.

McNeill, Lynne S. *Folklore Rules: A Fun, Quick, and Useful Introduction to the Field of Academic Folklore Studies*. Utah State University Press, 2013.

TEXT, TEXTURE, AND CONTEXT

According to my mentor Alan Dundes, each concept of the trinity of text, texture, and context allows us to engage in a separate but interrelated level of analysis of folklore. Just using one wouldn't get us as far as using all three in unison.

So let's start with text. Dundes refers to text as "essentially a version or a single telling of a tale, a recitation of a proverb, a singing of a folksong [sic]" (23). In folklore studies we often use "text," "item," and "version" interchangeable, to refer to that single instance of a recognizable bit of folklore manifesting in the world. Text stands in contrast to genre, which is a grouping of like items. For example, joke is a genre; that one knock-knock joke about interrupting cows is a text, while the one about a starfish would be another text. The Grimms' "Cinderella" is a text, while fairy tale is the genre.

One thing that often confuses students is that due to secondary school English education, many of them associate "text" with the text of a poem, play, novel, or short story – in other words, a textual artifact that is linguistic, published, and unchanging. None of which necessarily apply to folklore. So there's often a bit of resistance or confusion when I want to talk about the text of a material culture item (such as a dance costume, which is one of the material culture genres I study), or a superstition as a text. For instance, in the dance form I perform, I usually wear what in FatChance BellyDance style we call a "hair garden" (folk speech text right there), whereas the whole assemblage of my costume could be considered one coherent text worthy of documentation and study, since it reveals so very much about my individual and group identity. These uses of "text" are all legit in folklore studies, so I require my students to learn them.

By the same token, if it's too abstract for you to describe the text of an item of folklore, well, you might not be dealing with folklore at all, but rather some general realm of culture. Or you might be a passive bearer of that genre, not quite familiar enough with it to properly classify it.

As we'll see throughout this book, verbal folklore texts are generally translatable (it's easy to translate the plot of a story) while their texture and context may be more dependent on linguistic or cultural markers that don't always translate easily. When it comes to material culture and customary folklore, texts also tend to translate: a basket is a basket in most other contexts, gestures are recognizable as meaningful even if their meaning isn't apparent, and so on.

Documenting the text is always the first step in folklore analysis. No text = nothing to discuss.

Next up, texture. According to Dundes, the texture of an item of folklore is its set of unique stylistic features or markers. With verbal folklore (such as narratives or jokes) this would mean its language and linguistic features. Some genres of folklore with highly distinctive phrasing are accordingly more difficult to translate (think tongue twisters or proverbs vs. jokes and fairy tales, which travel more freely as evidenced by the fact that every culture has its own linguistic version of "Once upon a time").

The analysis of texture is complicated by the fact that it's not always going to distinguish genres from one another. Dundes points out: "Rhyme is a textural feature of some proverbs, but the fact that rhyme is also found in some riddles means that it is of limited value in distinguishing a proverb from a riddle" (23).

This is where it becomes important to utilize texture in conjunction with the other two levels of analysis, text and context. Texture is often inseparable from the text; we can talk about rhyme or alliteration abstractly, but seeing how they actually play out in a verbal item of folklore is a different experience. Some genres tend to have rigid textures (as with formulaic genres like proverbs, riddles, and Q&A jokes), while others are quite loose. Context can impact texture as when people swap in or out coarse language for various audiences.

Before winding this portion of the chapter down, I want to note that most folklore has a unique texture that sets it apart from the rest of daily life. Just think of the English-language words that perhaps most connote a fairy tale: *Once upon a time.*

See, fairy tales are hugely recognizable, in large part because of their texture. As I wrote in a post listing off a bunch of fairy-tale features:[1]

> Fairy tales have a distinctive style that tends toward simplicity and abstraction (Swiss folklorist Max Lüthi has written extensively on this topic). In English, we

recognize many linguistic markers of fairy tales: once upon a time, happily ever after, as golden as the sun, and so on. Fairy tales speak in metaphors, and as such, their language tends to favor extremes (not just black, but black as a raven's feather), symmetry, and synecdoche.

How do you know you're about to listen to a fairy tale, or read a comic book version, or watch a TV or movie adaptation of one? There's usually some textural framing going on, the iconic "Once upon a time" opener or a riff on it.

Similarly, when someone says "A priest and a rabbi walk into a bar…" they've just introduced texture into the conversation that, in the English language, connotes that a joke is about to follow. Granted, texture isn't a universal (but what is?!) since different regions have different jokes, and so on.

Many kinds of folklore are set apart from mundane life by texture. Whether it's the special preparations that mark off a holiday weekend, or the literal texture that is often present on a historical folk costume, we're attuned on some level to texture as a differentiating quality of culture. Again, it changes between regions and eras and subcultures, but if you start thinking about it, you could probably list off some textural features of folklore texts that you're familiar with.

Finally, we move on to context. As Alan Dundes writes: "The context of an item is the specific social situation in which that particular item is actually employed" (23). In theory, the context can be observed by anyone, since it has objective elements to it, such as the location, time of day, the number of participants, and so on. But there are also subjective parts, things that only cultural insiders or members of a folk group would know.

Since context is something we observe on the ground, as it's happening, Dundes notes that it's important to distinguish context from function. As I've written, function encompasses the role that folklore performs in society, such as education or validation of norms. You need context in order to grasp function, since function doesn't happen in a vacuum, but they're not the same thing. Both function and context have to do with the larger social scale of folklore, but context is observable on the ground, therefore making it somewhat more objective, while function must be extrapolated (based on interview data and the folklorist's interpretation thereof; sometimes members of a folk group also can elucidate how a given folklore text functions for them).

Context matters more for some genres than others. Dundes goes so far as to write that "contextless jokes are of limited value to the social scientist" (26). What he means by this is that jokes so often deal with taboo topics that if we don't know when they're deemed appropriate or acceptable, we're missing out on a big chunk of the overall picture. Because folklore always reflects culture on some level, we need to be able to connect the dots between the content (as seen in the text) and context of folklore items to understand them.

But in general, we want context to pair with every folklore text. We want to know how texture relates, too. You can't define a folklore genre solely based on texture or context; for example, both jokes and urban legends are often told in informal settings, and both tend to have iconic introductions, but that doesn't make them the same thing at all.

When it comes to recording context if you're doing fieldwork, you can never be too detailed. Make note of every detail as though you're answering the basic questions of journalism (who, what, where, when, why, and how). Distinguish between the specifics that you observe yourself, and those you have to ask others for. You can always pare down the details later if you're writing your fieldwork observations into a paper or article, but you can't go back to the original context to revisit it... at least not until we invent time travel or get a better handle on virtual reality!

Welcome to the useful trinity of text, texture, and context. If you're a student in one of my folklore classes, I've just handed you a cheat-sheet to doing well. For everyone else, I imagine these concepts are useful in a number of venues!

References:

Dundes, Alan. "Texture, Text, and Context." *Interpreting Folklore*, Indiana University Press, 1980, 20-32.

THE FUNCTIONS OF FOLKLORE

In the section intro for "genres," I introduce my four-part rubric (content, context, form, and function) and say that I will go into more detail about function elsewhere. Well, that's happening here.

First, we need to disambiguate "function" since it can have a couple of meanings in academic folklore and anthropology contexts. What I mean in this chapter is function as the purpose, intention, meaning, or effect of a given folklore item or performance. You might also run across function as a plot point in a fairy tale, in the legacy of Soviet structuralist scholar Vladimir Propp. Finally, you might have heard of the anthropological school of thought called functionalism, which was all about the functions of given parts of a society in relation to the organic whole.

Anyway, the functions I'm talking about here are the roles that folklore can play in society, basically the "why" of why people transmit, perform, remember, and transform folklore.

In this field, we tend to talk about there being four major

functions of folklore, thanks to the scholarship of William Bascom, a major mid-century folklorist.

Before I go into Bascom's list of four functions, we have to cover function zero, the assumed function of all folklore. That function can be described as entertainment, fun, laughter, and joy. That's just like…duh. If folklore is expressive culture, then it's going to be marked off, or textured differently, from the rest of speech, social acts, and general everyday culture. When people launch into a joke or legend or proverb or some other form of verbal folklore, there are usually shifts in language to indicate that they're now in a special realm of culture. There can be explicit verbal framing, such as "Did you hear the one about…?" or "OMG, this happened to a friend of a friend…" The framing is different in material culture and customary folklore, but it's there nonetheless.

So if a student writes that one of the functions of folklore is entertainment on their exam, they don't get points for it. That's a built-in function of folklore. It's a given. It's obvious that one of the reasons folklore exists is to sprinkle a little novelty into daily life. That's why one of the definitions of folklore is "artistic communication in small groups." It's not just any communication, but *artistic* communication, marked off as different than every other word we utter for communicative purposes, or every other act we do just to get through the day.

(This also plays into one of my folklore pet peeves: when people think folklore is "just fun" or "just entertaining." Say that to a folklorist if you want to watch our faces turn red as we bite back a number of highly amusing expletives.)

Okay, on to Bascom's list. The four main functions of folklore are:

- Education
- Validation of culture and social norms
- Maintaining conformity and exerting social pressure
- Providing a release, outlet, or wish fulfillment

To illustrate these functions, fairy tales come to mind (my mind, at least) as the perfect example, since they can fulfill all four functions in various contexts (and of course, they're entertaining, fulfilling function zero). Fairy tales educate about gender roles, demonstrating how masculinity and femininity are supposed to be enacted. Fairy tales validate the existence of property-based and inheritance wealth systems. Fairy tales exert social pressure to marry, monogamously and heterosexually. And finally, fairy tales provide wish fulfillment in giving the plucky protagonist their happily ever after, complete with marriage and ascension to the throne.

Not all genres of folklore touch equally on each of these functions, though traces of them tend to weave throughout most folklore. Jokes tend to be heavy on the release/outlet/wish fulfillment end of the spectrum, for example. Myths are especially important for validation of culture and social norms, as well as revealing why those norms exist in relation to the broader culture and whom they serve, as per the culture reflector theory, or the classic folkloristic/anthropological theory that folklore and expressive culture essentially reflect major elements of that culture.

Context is also important here. As Lynne McNeill observes:

> [T]he same piece of folklore can serve multiple functions at once. An urban legend can serve as a warning for a whole community or simply as a psychological release

> for an anxious individual. A political joke can allow an adult to test the leanings of a social gathering, or it can allow a young person to unofficially push against parental ideology. A folk song can serve as a literal commentary on current or historical events, or as a symbolic expression of complex emotion. A customary holiday game or sporting event can provide social release as well as reinforce a group's identity. (31)

So, the list of functions is ever-expanding and in flux, because among the four up top, you probably didn't see "reinforce group identity," but that is acknowledged as a hugely important function of folklore in current scholarship. I often refer to folklore as "social glue" in a shorthand way of describing how folklore can reflect, create, and reinforce group identity (but it can also reflect individual identity too, so the relationship of folklore to identity is quite complex). This is a bit of a side note, too, but the more I learn about trauma, the more I think folklore serves a number of functions in understanding and addressing trauma. Some therapists believe that merely narrating one's trauma is an effective way of healing it (i.e., personal narrative serves a therapeutic function), while others claim that revisiting a traumatic incident verbally before one feels bodily safe can be triggering and retraumatizing. Bessel Van der Kolk sums up these various approaches in his book *The Body Keeps the Score,* and I bring up these examples here to suggest that narrating one's story may serve therapeutic functions in some situations but not universally.

The main point is that folklore has a purpose, and our job as folklore scholars is to uncover that purpose and thus contextualize folklore as one of the main communicative tools that humans have.

References:

Bascom, William. "Four Functions of Folklore." *The Journal of American Folklore* vol. 67, no. 266, 1954, pp. 333-349.

McNeill, Lynne S. *Folklore Rules: A Fun, Quick, and Useful Introduction to the Field of Academic Folklore Studies*. Utah State University Press, 2013.

FIELDWORK

WHERE DOES FOLKLORE COME FROM? How do scholars get our greedy little paws on it? One of the main answers to this question is: fieldwork.

I'm an introvert, so I'd almost always rather hide out in an archive than have to go interact with people, but where do archives get their information? Fieldwork. Folklore books? Also fieldwork. Even if you're just learning the basics so you understand the study of folklore better, it's essential to have an idea of what fieldwork is and how we generally go about it.

See, folklore doesn't exist in a vacuum. It doesn't simply fall from the sky (instead of "It's Raining Men," how about "It's Raining Urban Legends"?!). Because we can think of folklore as informally transmitted traditional culture, or artistic communication in small groups, or creativity in everyday life, that means folklore happens in the interactions between people…usually face-to-face and live, but not always. So we need some way of capturing those interactions, figuring out what counts as folklore texts (more on "text" as a concept in an earlier chapter), and sifting through those recordings and notes to make sense of them.

Before recording technologies were accessible, it was common for folklorists to interview cultural specialists such as taletellers and try to write down what they were hearing as quickly as possible, sometimes using specialized notation techniques. The Grimm brothers, for example, famously interviewed a number of women they knew in the early 1800s in order to collect folktales and fairy tales from them...but what's less commonly known is that the Grimms violated one of our modern-day rules of folklore collection and changed their materials in the process of publishing them. We're not always going to like what we find while doing fieldwork, but that shouldn't stop us from reporting truthfully on it, unless it would put our collaborators in danger, which is a whole other bag of ethical dilemmas we regularly address.

Fieldwork is a technique that folklorists have in common with anthropologists and others in the social sciences. We need data, our preferred form of data comes from people, so we go out and interact with those people. In this sense, fieldwork is contiguous with ethnography, a term that means the description and/or writing of culture. Fieldwork is what you do, ethnography is what you produce (or at least, that's the way I think about it; it's certainly not the only way to differentiate the two).

When I teach fieldwork techniques, I emphasize conducting interviews, since it's an artificial set-up but it tends to be something everyone can successfully do. Obviously it's better to have obtained everyone's consent previously to record them and just *happen to* stumble upon an amazing session of joke-telling, ballad-singing, or what-have-you...but it doesn't always work out that way in real life, unless you're doing long-term fieldwork with a given folk group. Consent is another important thing here: if you're just doing a folklore collection for a class project that only your professor will read, you're probably fine just getting your collaborators' verbal consent, but if you're intending to produce actual scholarship (a conference paper, article, and/or book), you'll likely need to go through your university's Institutional Review Board or IRB, since any scholarly work with human subjects must be reviewed to make sure it's not harmful or exploitative. Study up on medical history if you're curious why this is a thing (start with the history of gynecology or the Tuskegee syphilis experiment).

I like the fieldwork tips on the website hosted by Traditional Arts Indiana,[1] though there are whole books on how to conduct folklore fieldwork, and I took a graduate course on it too. Lynne McNeill, as usual, has a great segment in it on *Folklore Rules* where she gives suggestions for how to conduct folklore fieldwork in case you have a school assignment requiring it, or in case your interest is piqued and you want to, say, document your family's stories. She highlights the importance of not simply recording or jotting down what people are saying, but also taking note of the entire social context, and questioning your own assumptions going in:

> Paying attention to the ways people interact, both with each other and with the space they're in, provides lots of opportunities for identifying the unspoken cultural knowledge that people are putting to use in a given situation. The practice of ethnographic observation often involves consideration of both emic (insider) and etic

(outsider) perspectives, which can require seeing familiar situations in a new light. (26)

This is crucial advice because your degree of insider-ness vs. outsider-ness can both impact the kinds of data you're getting in your fieldwork *and* your interpretation of it. A century ago, it was a common rite of passage for folklorists and anthropologists to try to go abroad and study "exotic" and "foreign" people for their graduate fieldwork (yes, gag, that sort of colonialist mindset has been heavily interrogated since then), and in those cases, outsiders are both a bit more clueless going in and more likely to catch things that insiders might take for granted. Similarly, studying one's own culture using scholarly tools has its advantages - you probably already have "ins" with these people - but also disadvantages, like if you can't get enough critical distance to really analyze what's happening in front of you. All fieldwork, I think, has us toggling between intimacy and distance as a way to try to understand humanity better. Hopefully we acknowledge our own inevitably biases in doing so, too; there's no such thing as true neutral when it comes to humanity.

In his touching essay "Folklore's Four Sisters,"[2] folklorist Steve Zeitlin of City Lore classifies fieldwork as the "body" of folklore practice, using a four-part metaphor:

The *body* might be thought of as the body of work, the documentation–the stories, oral histories, and materials collected in the field. The *mind* is the scholarship or the interpretation of the documentation. The *heart* of the field is activism and empathy, central to the work of

> folklorists who collaborate with communities and individuals to amplify their voices and provide them with venues, resources, and ways to supplement their livelihoods. Perhaps, the *soul* of the field is the creative artistry embodied by the talented people with whom we work and collaborate–as well as our own artistic sensibility that we bring to the task.

Zeitlin goes on to describe a number of pioneers in the field who are excellent fieldworkers but also combine their fieldwork with activist and/or artistic sensibilities. The fantastic online archive of folklore documentaries at FolkStreams.net gets a shout-out too, and it's well worth checking out if you want to see some of the filmic results of folklore fieldwork.

These days, we're using more digital tools than ever to conduct fieldwork; I've interviewed people over Skype and over email, and of course it's easier than ever before to record interviews. As a dance scholar, I am thrilled that there are so many ways now to visually capture dance that are more accessible and don't require, like, learning Labanotation (look it up for a fun ride through attempts to transcribe dance movements before video cameras were common). But with the increase in digital tools we also get challenges such as new ethical implications about when it is and isn't okay to record people doing folkloric things in public.

The American Folklife Center at the Library of Congress is doing great work with existing fieldwork collections, and I've heard from my friends working there that they're also addressing some of these ethical issues around collecting and archiving folklore. Look them up[3]...you can browse some of their collections online and check out their front-page educational resources which include a bunch of fieldwork tips.

References:

McNeill, Lynne S. *Folklore Rules: A Fun, Quick, and Useful Introduction to the Field of Academic Folklore Studies*. Utah State University Press, 2013.

WORLDVIEW

WHY DO folklorists bother studying expressive culture? It turns out that we're looking for insights into worldview, or what people believe to be true about the world. And that's very valuable indeed.

According to my mentor, Alan Dundes, the search for data on worldview is in fact a key reason to study folklore specifically. He writes:

> No genre of folklore is so trivial or insignificant that it cannot provide important data for the study of worldview. Worldview, the way a people perceives the world and its place in it, permeates all aspects of a given culture and this is why the pattern of the whole is to be found even in that whole's smallest part. Yet it is not always easy to discern patterns of a worldview, especially when one attempts to look at a culture as a whole. Methodologically, it makes more sense to

> examine microcosms, and from these examinations, one may have better access to the corresponding macrocosm. (83)

First, that paragraph gives a good definition of worldview: the way a folk group perceives the world and their place in it. To this, I would add that worldview encompasses factors like morality, causality, ethics, aesthetics, and more. Our worldview is what tells us what is good, right, and beautiful in the world; what makes the sun rise and set; what happens after we die; who deserves access to which resources; and perhaps even who deserves violence.

Next, Dundes presents the idea there's a definite relationship between culture, folklore, and underlying values. Those of us in folklore and anthropology hint at this in the culture reflector theory, which I sum up as follows:

> With our inquisitive fingers on this popular pulse, folklorists can analyze the deep connections between folklore and culture, aiming to understand the values beneath the stories. Folklore may not be an exact mirror of culture, but it certainly reflects culture on some level, and discerning the ripples and patterns of that reflection can lead to important insights on a societal scale.[1]

Finally, linking folklore with worldview provides ammunition against the argument that much folklore is too trivial to be taken seriously. That's an important if obvious point to make, since when I tell people I study folklore, there's still occasionally an eyeroll response, as in, how could that be worthy of your time?! No aspect of human behavior is too trivial for study, I say, and those denigrating folklore should think long and hard about their own hobbies, pleasures, and social habits before judging those of other people.

Let's move on to a case study. In "As the Crow Flies: A Straightforward Study of Lineal Worldview in American Folk-speech," Dundes takes folk speech as his topic, and compiles an extensive list of all the things Americans say involving lines vs. circles. Examples include:

- being straight with someone vs. being round-about
- thinking straight vs. circular reasoning
- being fair and square vs. wheeling and dealing

There are plenty more texts in the article. In his analysis, Dundes suggests that Americans "perceive both time and space in lineal terms" (208). Our perception of history as a forward-moving progression, and our division of space into rectilinear forms, may say more about us than about how the world truly is. Of course the truth is probably a bit more nuanced than that, but I tend to assign this essay by Dundes because I think it helps show one avenue that folklorists can take to work on worldview.

In theory we can study worldview using any genre of folklore (or combining multiple genres, as I did in my keynote on the body in folklore[2]). However, the use of folk speech to illustrate worldview is appropriate; as folklorist Barre Toelken observes: "A language not only communicates; it articulates a worldview" (22).

Again, you don't have to go all Sapir-Whorf hypothesis (the idea that the language we learn literally structures our brains and hence our sense of reality) to understand that the language we speak and the folklore we perform both shapes and reflects our values. And this is a huge reason we study folklore: to help articulate cultural senses or understandings that people may not be able to consciously speak, but which compel them to act nonetheless.

References:

Dundes, Alan. "Pecking Chickens: A Folk Toy as a Source for the Study of Worldview." *Folklore Matters*, The University of Tennessee Press, 1989, 83-91.

—. "As the Crow Flies: A Straightforward Study of Lineal Worldview in American Folkspeech." *The Meaning of Folklore: The Analytical Essays of Alan Dundes*, edited by Simon J. Bronner, Utah State University Press, 2007, 196-210.

Toelken, Barre. *The Dynamics of Folklore. Revised and Expanded Edition*. Utah State University Press, 1996.

GENRE

GENRE IS, as its most basic, a way of categorizing folklore items based on how they are similarly structured. Lynne McNeill puts it like this:

> Rather than simply being the general shared awareness of how to behave in a group or a society, folklore comprises the specific expressive forms that a group uses to communicate and interact. We call these forms the genres of folklore, and just as literature students study different genres of literature (poems, plays, novellas) or film students study different genres of film (drama, comedy, action-adventure), folklorists study different genres of folklore, such as customs, narratives, and beliefs. (5)

As McNeill notes, genre relates to the "lore" side of folklore. Recall that a folk group is any group of people with a shared identity or a characteristic in common; thus it follows that folklore is the lore – or expressive forms a.k.a. genres – of a given folk group, whether it's college students or Asian Americans or LGBTQ folks (or someone who occupies all three of those identities).

However, folklorists don't own the concept of genre. As Trudier Harris-Lopez points out, the term originally comes from Latin and means "kind" or "sort," and thus we find genre as a classificatory term used in many other academic disciplines and popular discourses. Books, TV shows, and films get sorted by genre; clothing and food too, to a degree. So while folklorists use *genre* specifically within our discipline to refer to how expressive culture takes traditionally-recognized shapes, and tends to get funneled into those shapes since they're what people already know and respond to, we don't have sole claim to the word.

At the same time, the pervasiveness of the concept of genre has been a tool that we've used to legitimize our discipline. Harris-Lopez writes:

> If folklorists could show that there were forms, traditions, events, practices, and narratives that could not fit comfortably into the purview of any other discipline, they would go a long way toward carving out the space they needed to conduct their field research and library work and earn their academic credibility. Isolating distinctive forms and articulating how folklorists' training was essential to understanding them led folklorists to adopt a broad-based concept of genre. A

> slippery concept, genre was nonetheless a crucial starting point for a discipline that was at times itself rather less than firm. (101)

I haven't nerded out about the history of folklore studies as much as I want to in this chapter, but Harris-Lopez is spot on here. The study of folklore has been notoriously difficult to define for over two centuries, and thus genre often seems like a great concept to latch on to, since we can say things like "Hey, no one's studying these genres, which don't quite fall into literature and also don't exactly fit into pop culture. We got this!" And because people recognize that genres exist in other areas of life, our claims resonate with people.

In fact, knowing about genres is useful precisely because they are so prevalent. They structure expectations for all sorts of daily interactions, some of which are folkloric in nature and others less so. From how you compose a text message to how you read your internet bill, genre prevails. Fairy-tale scholars Christine A. Jones and Jennifer Schacker expand on this analogy:

> Each of these communicative forms, which we might call "genres," is associated with a certain set of interpretive conventions; for instance, one doesn't expect metaphors and symbols to be part of the phone bill, nor does one expect a full, verifiable, and accurate account of current world events in response to a casual salutation ("Hi.").
>
> In fact, we are often only made aware of generic expectations when they are violated, when something

occurs that feels out of place, unexpected, even bizarre. (493)

Jones and Schacker are right: we steer our social interactions according to subtle genre cues, which we could *probably* articulate if we had to, but usually we don't. This is because many of us are passive bearers of conversational genres like folk speech and other types of language / linguistic folklore; we understand the rules inherently, but might have trouble pulling out principles and examples of why and how they work. Of course, coming up with counter-examples, the violations of which Jones and Schacker wrote, are often a good place to start. We all know it'd be ludicrous to shelve *50 Shades of Grey* with children's books or cookbooks, and we know this because we understand how literary genres work.

To bring the conversation back to folklore genres specifically, we tend to categorize genres of folklore into three or four overarching categories, in terms of how they're transmitted. I use the tripartite model of things people say (verbal folklore), things people do (customary folklore), and things people make (material culture). McNeill uses four categories and breaks them down as such:

- things we say (like jokes, songs, folktales, myths, and legends)
- things we do (like calendar customs, rituals, games, and rites of passage)
- things we make (like handmade objects, collections and assemblages, and folk art)
- things we believe (like superstitions, supernatural creatures, and folk religion) (38)

Folklorists often center their work around a series of bigger, more universally-known genres. At folklore conferences you'll almost always find a panel on folk narrative, for example. But there are always smaller genres, genres that are only locally known, too. If you can demonstrate that a genre has content, context, form/structure, and function (to use what I call the four-part rubric for analyzing genre) distinct from other genres in existence, then you may be onto something. But since we've been studying genre for over two centuries now, you're probably only going to discover a new genre if you're actually documenting something that is new in existence, like if a new folk group comes into being and expresses itself in a radical way.

To conclude, most folklorists engage with genre in one way or another. Ask a folklorist what she studies, and you may well get a list of genres as your answer. We retain it as a useful concept to categorize the lore that is informally transmitted across, between, and among folk groups, and we like that it has cultural currency elsewhere too.

References:

Harris-Lopez, Trudier. "Genre." *Eight Words for the Study of Expressive Culture*, edited by Burt Feintuch, University of Illinois Press, 2003, 99-120.

Jones, Christine A. and Jennifer Schacker. "On Fairy Tales and Their Anthologies." *Marvelous Transformations: An Anthology of Fairy Tales and Contemporary Critical Perspectives*, edited by Christine A. Jones and Jennifer Schacker, Broadview Press, 2013, 493-498.

McNeill, Lynne S. *Folklore Rules: A Fun, Quick, and Useful Introduction to the Field of Academic Folklore Studies*. Utah State University Press, 2013.

FOLK GROUP

For a long time, folklorists studied "the folk," that is to say, people who were distinctly Not Like Us: peasants, savages, children, and so on. Thankfully, that's changed.

In 2016 I started a blog post series called #FolkloreThursday, a nod to the Twitter hashtag that had become (and still is!) popular. In one of those posts[1] I described the origins of the term "folklore," coined by British scholar William Thoms in 1846. The suggestion that folklore is the study of the lore of the folk means we have to define two things (folk and lore) as well as their intersection. It's generally agreed that "lore" in this case means informally transmitted traditional knowledge, behaviors, texts, stories, artifacts, and customs… but then what makes lore into folklore?

If you flip through old issues of the Journal of American Folklore, the academic journal of the American Folklore Society (founded in 1888) you'd think that the "folk" are primarily primitives, peasants, and non-whites. It feels kinda creepy, racist, and classist to see article after article focusing on the folklore of Native Americans, African Americans – though not using that term if that gives you any idea – and various island peoples. This fit in with general trends in the academy as well as cultural anthropology specifically from the early 20th century, where the culture of Those People Over There was seen as more suited for study than the Things We Civilized People Do. Still sorta gross, but yay context?

Over time, the views shifted. Maaaaaybe we city-dwellers have folklore too (a trend that started, I believe, with the study of urban children's folklore and expanded from there, since doncha know kids are basically savages). Perhaps folklore isn't just the purview of the irrational non-Westerner. Perhaps it's something everyone engages in.

The shift in the meaning of "the folk" culminated in 1965 with Alan Dundes's essay "Who Are the Folk?" In it, he describes the historical connotations of "folk" and suggests a new direction. One key tidbit is that the folk were contrasted with the elite, such that the folk were always a dependently defined entity:

> The folk were understood to be a group of people who constituted the lower stratum, the so-called "vulgus in populo" – in contrast to the upper stratum or elite of that society … Folk as an old fashioned segment living on the margins of civilization was and for that matter still is equated to the concept of peasant. (2)

So we've got connotations of people who are peasants, illiterate (either pre-literate or non-literate), underdeveloped, rural… it's not pretty. But it's also part of our scholarly history.

Thankfully, Dundes decided to ditch the ethnocentric implication of the word "folk" and redefine it, saying that the object of study of folklorists is the lore of a given folk group. A folk group is any group of people with at least one common factor. That factor could be nationality, language, religion (which tends to make for a large folk group), or it could be something shared by fewer people, such as a hobby, family ties, or a small region/neighborhood. Not every folk group has face-to-face contact, though many do, but most of them will share a common core of folklore, even if not every member knows every item.

Further, most folk groups have both institutional and less-institutional facets to them, and it's that latter part that we're most interested in. As Lynne McNeill writes:

> Many of these groups clearly have an institutional culture as well as a folk culture – campuses, churches, occupations, states, and nations will have both official and unofficial aspects of their culture – and when we refer to those groups as a "folk group," we're purposefully focusing on their unofficial realm. In contrast, some groups don't have much of an institutional culture at all – friend groups and families are typically entirely folk or informal in their cultural existence and expression. It's a useful distinction to make, especially when seeking to avoid the "Folklore is everything!" fallacy. (5)

Anyway, back to the folk group. This is a major concept in folklore studies, and one I drill into my students' heads at the beginning of each semester. Folklore isn't just that old-timey peasant stuff, it's alive and something we all participate in. We each belong to multiple folk groups, sometimes overlapping, sometimes with similar shared values and sometimes with quite contradictory ones. Having the language to describe your group membership and resulting worldviews is a useful tool in understanding how social groups both shape and reflect your individual experiences.

Some folk groups are huge, with numbers in the millions. Others may be tiny, composed of just a handful of people. If a group has some identity in common, it's likely that they then generate shared folklore in whatever format makes the most sense for that group (for example, people who play online games together are more likely to have folk speech and other verbal folklore genres in common than material culture, but you never know!).

I'll conclude with a list of some folk groups that you may belong to…the fun thing is, the list of potential folk groups is ever-expanding, since the ways in which humans interact is also expanding!

- A family group (biological family, married-into family, chosen family)
- A religious group
- A nation, ethnicity, and / or linguistic group
- A group of students and / or teachers on the same campus
- Any type of hobby or crafting group
- A gaming group (online and / or in-person)
- A group that studies, practices, and / or performs an art form (musicians, dancers, stand-up comedians, and so on)

- A group of people who share a gender identity and/or sexuality (I'm fascinated by the folklore of sexual subcultures, for example, like swingers, polyamorous people, and other ethically non-monogamous folk)
- A group with something bodily in common (tattooed people could be considered a folk group, as could tattoo artists; disabled people may also be a folk group, and from what I've heard from disabled friends, while their conditions may vary, their personal narratives around botched medical treatment often share similar themes)
- I'm sure I missed some examples of folk groups… feel free to reach out on Twitter and let me know of examples that come to mind for you! (@foxyfolklorist)

References:

Dundes, Alan. "Who are the Folk?" *Essays in Folkloristics,* Rajkamal Electric Press, 1978, 1-21.

McNeill, Lynne S. *Folklore Rules: A Fun, Quick, and Useful Introduction to the Field of Academic Folklore Studies.* Utah State University Press, 2013.

ACTIVE VS. PASSIVE BEARERS

ARE you the person who always messes up the punchline of a joke? You, friend, might be a passive bearer of folklore.

Now that we have a more nuanced understanding of what folk groups are from the previous chapter, we can dig a little deeper and ask what distinguishes the people in folk groups from one another. Who are the ones who stand out as superb storytellers and joke tellers? Who are the ones making sure there's someone to carry on their legacy of the particular type of holiday food, or body art, or narrative?

We have Swedish folklorist Carl von Sydow to thank for the concept of active and passive bearers, which addresses these questions. Not everyone in a folk group engages with folklore in the same level; folk groups are rarely homogeneous. What's actually going on is that some people are deeply familiar with given folklore genres and items, and others are only passingly aware of them. We call these people active and passive bearers, and identifying them lets us get deeper into the "how" and "why" of folklore transmission.

An active bearer (or carrier) of a folklore genre actually tells the tales, sings the songs, and cooks the traditional holiday foods. They know the recipes, the methods, the ritual formulas. They're not always seen as performers, but they're often held in high esteem in a community. In contrast, the passive bearers will recognize the folklore when it's told, performed, or created, but they won't necessarily be able to replicate it. It's common for active bearers to be the ones involved in bringing folklore to new regions and groups, or to help document and preserve it for future generations.

The distinction isn't always helpful for studying/documenting every genre of folklore, though. As Alan Dundes explains:

> Von Sydow's distinction appears more applicable to folklore genres that require considerable artistic expertise, such as epics, folktales, and folksongs. It seems less useful for minor genres such as folk speech or gestures where in theory any member of a culture can "perform." The distinction is also useful for prospective folklore scholars who should obviously seek out the active bearers in the community to serve as informants. To be sure, passive bearers might also be interviewed, not so much to elicit texts but rather to learn what texts might possibly mean. A passive bearer might not have told a tale, but he or she, having heard the tale repeatedly might have an opinion as to the tale's meaning(s). (139)

Why this matters:

- It directs us to people who are more likely to be intimately familiar with the genre, so that we can do a better job of collecting folklore in the field.
- We can bring a personal element to the study of folklore, and gain more information about a tradition bearer's life context and how that might impact their engagement with a given genre.
- Finally, folklorists are all about studying tradition in various contexts: what makes it work? What makes it thrive? And one of the best concepts we have to do so is that of active and passive bearers, because it reminds us that folk groups are not monolithic, and different people engage with tradition differently.

Now that you know about this key concept, can you identify any folklore genres of which you're an active or passive bearer?

References:

Dundes, Alan, editor. *International Folkloristics: Classic Contributions by the Founders of Folklore*. Rowman & Littlefield Publishers Inc., 1999.

VERSION VS. VARIANT

By now you should understand that folklorists are practically obsessed with variation. But when we call something a variant, it has a really specific meaning.

Variation is key to understanding folklore as a process of informal cultural transmission. No official or institutional oversight means that folklore is free to proliferate in variants, though of course there are cultural constraints on the "right" version of something. However, we use all these terms in slightly different ways. This led Alan Dundes to make his famously puzzling remark: "Thus all variants must by definition be versions, but not all versions are necessarily variants" (290, note 6).

Let's unpack that! (To the soundtrack of fellow Dundes students cackling about the times we've put this on a folklore exam as a true/false question; you know who you are)

First, recall that folklorists call individual items of folklore texts. And we apply this word to any item of expressive culture, broadening the connotation of literary texts as fixed written things, so we have texts that are verbal in nature, like a single fairy tale or legend; those that are customary like a ritual practice; and those that are material, like the recipe for a dish or an item of adornment.

We tend to use "text," "item," and "version" interchangeably when describing *this one piece of folklore I collected/found in an archive/encountered online/etc.* But when we want to specifically talk about the kinds of variation we're encountering, we will often use variant, which implies greater fluidity and flexibility in the nature of the item, rather than the fixity that text tends to connote.

As Lynne McNeill demonstrates, it's key to use our terms in a way that foregrounds the importance of variation: "the lore, the stuff that's being passed around (which could be stories, customs, beliefs, whatever) isn't limited to a single correct version. When a cultural expression is (re)created anew each time it gets shared, it varies a bit, and it's this variation that allows us to identify a particular cultural form as folklore" (11).

It's important to keep in mind that folklorists usually aren't interested in being the One True Version police. While we find it endlessly fascinating when other people debate whether someone messed up a joke or told the "right" ending to a fairy tale, we're not usually professionally invested in this question of correctness (though personally, it may be another matter entirely!).

So if we use "version" to mean "any iteration of a folklore text," why do we also need "variant" as a term? It's because while variation is key to folklore in general, not every text is going to vary significantly from other texts of the same joke / proverb / custom / whatever.

This is one reason why we have the distinction between

free-phrase and fixed-phrase texts. If you collect ten proverb texts from ten different people, and nine of them have exactly the same phrasing, while one differs a little, then you've got ten versions comprised of two variants: the type with the more commonly-found phrasing, and that one outlier. Or you could say we've got ten versions, including one variant, or here are nine identical versions and a variant. There's a little flexibility in how we use this language.

You could also picture this in terms of concentric circles: every version of a text is included in the larger circle, and those that depart from it in some fashion would have their own interior circles, showing that they're variants of the more mainstream or common form.

The version/variant distinction isn't limited to literal phrasing, either. If you have a handful of texts of "Little Red Riding Hood" where the woodcutter saves the girl and her grandma, and then one where the wolf just eats them both, end of story (as in Charles Perrault's 1697 published story), then they'd all be considered versions of ATU 333, but the Perrault text with its outlier of an ending would be called a variant.

This gets, uh, interesting because obviously the concept of variant is relative. You need to gather enough versions before labeling any variants in order to get a sense for their distribution. McNeill ties this back to some of our discipline's main concerns about transmission:

> Variation also implies another important marker of folklore: there has to be more than one version of something in order for it to vary. So in order to identify something as folklore, we have to find it in more than

> one place. Let's say that you write down a story in your secret journal that you never let anyone read. Even if it sounds like a folktale (with princesses and witches and fairy godmothers and magic mirrors) or sounds like an urban legend (with hook-handed maniacs and persecuted babysitters), it's not folklore until it's been passed along. Remember, identifying folklore is all about identifying how it travels; if it hasn't traveled at all, then it's simply not folklore. In fact, if it hasn't been shared, it's simply not "folk" - remember, "folk" implies "culture," which implies "group," not a single person. This is why we so often call folklore "traditional" - it gets passed on from person to person, leaving multiple versions in its wake. (12)

Thus the issue of even assembling enough versions to proclaim some of them variants relates to the central issues we study as folklorists: group identity, enculturation, tradition, and, of course, variation.

Say it with me: all variants are versions, but not all versions are variants. Hopefully now it makes sense!

References:

Dundes, Alan. *Interpreting Folklore*. Bloomington: Indiana University Press, 1980.

McNeill, Lynne S. *Folklore Rules: A Fun, Quick, and Useful Introduction to the Field of Academic Folklore Studies*. Boulder, Colorado: University Press of Colorado, 2013.

MOTIF VS. THEME

These two concepts are intertwined, but I'll start with motif since it's the smaller and more specific unit of the two. Since motifs show up everywhere in folk narrative, it's important to get a sense of how we use the term in folklore scholarship and how we incorporate motifs in our research.

Folklorist Stith Thompson defines motif as:

> A *motif* is the smallest element in a tale having a power to persist in tradition. In order to have this power it must have something unusual and striking about it. Most motifs fall into three classes. First are the actors in a tale – gods, or unusual animals, or marvelous creatures like witches, ogres, or fairies, or even conventionalized human characters like the favorite youngest child or the cruel stepmother. Second come certain items in the background of the action – magic objects, unusual customs, strange beliefs, and the like. In the third place

> there are single incidents – and these comprise the great majority of motifs. (415-416)

If you're a fan of TV tropes,[1] you can think of motifs as being like tropes: sometimes the simplest of details in a narrative, sometimes whole plot hooks. If it's a detail that can hop from one story to another in its entirety, then you've got a motif.

Motifs are usually explicit in a folk narrative text, meaning that they usually appear in the language that comprises the text. Got a story with a wicked witch? Guess what, you've got yourself a motif! It's also common to see motifs cluster by genre, as in, there are motifs you expect to see popping up more in fairy tales than in legends or myths, and so on.

How do we study motifs? By indexing them. Now, unlike the tale type index which solely classifies folktale plots, the motif index classifies motifs from all genres of folk narrative: folktale, myth, legend, epic, and so on. The system that Stith Thompson came up with when he published *The Motif-Index of Folk Literature* (1932-36) was to "bring together material from everywhere and arrange it by a logical system" (423). At first, this meant lots and lots of notecards, since this was done in the era before computers. Ultimately, Thompson's goal was "arranging and assorting narrative material so that it can be easily found" (424) rather than sorting materials by location or genre.

So, for example, you might look under category D for magic, or category E for the dead, if you want to learn about ghosts. Every letter of the alphabet is represented, with thousands of entries each, and with Z as the catch-all for miscellaneous motifs.

The body is a motif in many folk narrative texts and genres, which is something I nerded out about in my keynote on the body in folklore.[2] How body motifs are presented can tell us a lot about a given culture's values and worldview, their views on gender, and so on. Categorizing motifs can be an incredibly useful way for getting at how folklore functions, and the "why" of its transmission and performance, and so on.

The cool thing is, you can access an online version of the Motif at two university sites.[3] So don't take my word for it, go explore!

Okay, onto theme. Motif and theme go hand-in-hand in folklore studies, but theme in particular has a slightly different connotation than in daily or literary use. When I teach college-level folklore classes, I'm intent on my students understanding the difference between motif and theme, and how to use the terms properly to analyze folklore texts. The ability to do so demonstrates the key insight that what's found on the surface of folklore texts is only the tip of the iceberg.

Recall that a motif is "the smallest element in a tale having a power to persist in tradition." Motifs are almost always explicit at the textual level, that is, they appear word-for-word in the performance or transcription of the folk narrative (though it's worth noting that we also use these terms in discussing material culture, such as pottery; motifs would include the most prevalent designs such as spirals or depictions of animals).

In contrast, theme is the abstraction of a meaningful idea or message that the listener, viewer, or reader gleans from the folklore text, or which the teller/narrator might intend to convey. In addition to working with a single text, we can assemble a number of texts from a given genre, list their motifs, and then arrive at an understanding of the main themes that genre expresses.

For example, if I were to tell you some dumb blonde jokes, we'd end up with a list of motifs like hair color, mistakes, and stupid incidents/people. But if you look at the aggregate of dumb blonde jokes, as well as the cultural context in which they emerged, it becomes clear that they're really about gender. Nobody introduces a dumb blonde joke, however, by saying: "Here's a joke about gender conflict in contemporary American culture..." For the most part, when you're describing what a folklore text or genre is *about*, you're talking theme. And there are some narrators who will introduce story texts that way...but usually inferring the theme(s) of a text means doing a little digging.

One particularly intriguing case study when it comes to themes in folklore genres is personal narrative. Let's recall that despite their plots that are unique to the teller (being based on the teller's life experience), personal narratives count as folklore because they become traditional to the teller over time, and thus we can document multiple existence and variation at work (key hallmarks of folklore). The other important factor is that culture shapes what is deemed an acceptable or entertaining narrative, and thus we can document the existence of themes in personal narratives as another way to demonstrate their traditionality.

As personal narrative scholar Sandra Dolby points out, "the *use* of themes constitutes creative expressions" (24, italics in original). In other words, narrators deliberately inflect their narratives with themes, in order to convey a number of meanings. Further, there are three main kinds of themes that tend to be expressed in personal narratives:

> By creating a personal narrative, a storyteller articulates and affirms personal values along three thematic lines: (1) character, (2) behavior, and (3) attitude. The storyteller *chooses* events that illustrate themes of characterization, didactic themes (behavior), and humorous or ironic themes (attitude). The telling *is* the choosing of the theme and the creation of the event. (24)

As Dolby asserts, the literary goal of the personal narrative as an art form is to illustrate the teller's chosen theme, thus demonstrating something significant about the teller's personal (perhaps moral) character, or about what the teller's advice and values in a given situation are, or to convey the teller's attitude about a given topic. Obviously, these themes can be interwoven in the same narrative; advice dispensed with a humorous attitude might be an easier pill to swallow than solemnly (to the border of judgey) given advice.

Thus, with a genre like personal narrative that is more on the idiosyncratic and unique end of the traditionality spectrum (unlike narrative genres like folktale and legend where given plot types persist across centuries and language barriers), we can utilize themes to point out how personal narratives have folkloric qualities. In contemporary America, for example, we can identify the types of themes that many personal narratives display, which Dolby arranges according to her three thematic lines above:

> Among those reflecting characterization of the teller are (1) honesty, integrity; (2) cleverness, wit; (3) bravery,

> heroism, fearlessness; (4) practicality, business acuity; (5) charm, seductiveness; (6) loyalty, patriotism; (7) generosity or affection; and (8) manliness or maturity. Humorous themes are generally classifiable as involving (1) embarrassing situations, (2) ironic situations, or (3) incongruent occurrences. Homiletic themes intended to elucidate moral lessons are reflected in stories based upon (1) terrifying situations, war-time experience; (2) horrifying situations, cruel events; (3) unjust situations; (4) poignant situations; or (5) practical problems in managing one's affairs. (28)

These personal narrative themes are unique to this cultural context for a number of historical reasons. For example, Dolby was collecting folklore from people who were alive during the Great Depression, so it's no wonder that practicality and survival skills in the face of oppressively difficult situations would be considered narrative material; similarly, business acuity would be valued in capitalist societies, not necessarily ones with a difference economic system. Thus, an arrangement of personal narrative themes might look different coming from a different region or era.

If you were to collect personal narratives today, I bet that one or more of the themes listed above would emerge once you started to interpret the texts. Other themes not listed here might emerge as well, such as the tension between group identity and individual identity. Yes, we're in somewhat subjective territory, but stacking up enough texts with enough motifs will lead to some overlapping interpretations over time. Themes always exist in connection to the values of the groups and individuals articulating them. As Dolby writes: "Such themes are the narrative cores that tie the structural subtypes of the personal narrative to real functional concerns in culture and represent as well identifiable traditions useful in folklore classification" (28).

Every folklore genre has persistent themes that crop up and connect that genre back to the needs and concerns of a given folk group. These big-picture ideas, about what humanity is, what love is, what courage is, and so on, are central to artistic expressions, whether folkloric in nature or not. If there's no theme to dig a little deeper for, it's probably not going to be interesting enough artistically for people to latch onto it and transmit/engage with it.

References:

Dolby Stahl, Sandra. *Literary Folkloristics and the Personal Narrative*. Indiana University Press, 1989.

Thompson, Stith. *The Folktale*. University of California Press, 1977 [1946].

TALE TYPE

FOLKLORISTS LOVE CLASSIFYING THINGS, and our concept of type, specifically tale type, demonstrates this usefully.

In my chapter on the folktale, I mention tale types as distinct folktale plots that folklorists categorized by giving them numbers (in what is now the Aarne-Thompson-Uther or ATU index). To expand briefly on that explanation of type, I'll add some information from Stith Thompson – yes, the same Thompson whose name now appears in the type index because he was one of the main people who revised it. He wrote:

> A type is a traditional tale that has an independent existence. It may be told as a complete narrative and does not depend for its meaning on any other tale. It may indeed happen to be told with another tale, but the fact that it may appear alone attests its independence. It may consist of only one motif or many. Most animal tales

> and jokes and anecdotes are types of one motif. The ordinary *Märchen* (tales like Cinderella and Snow White) are types consisting of many of them. (415)

Motif is different than type (being the smallest unit of a unit that can persist over tradition), and I covered it in the previous chapter. The distinction can be a bit slippery, as some folktales are so short that the motif basically *is* the tale type, but this is usually not the case. Most types have multiple motifs associated with them; just think of Cinderella (ATU type 510A) and the glass slipper as recognition token, Little Red Riding Hood (type 333) and the color of her cloak plus the big bad wolf, and you get the idea.

While there are now tale type indexes for almost every major region of the world, the first type index, created in 1910 by Finnish folklorist Antti Aarne, was but one slim volume. Animal tales (like Aesop's fables) are numbers 1-299, fairy tales numbered 300-749, and so on from there, with other folktales numbering up into the thousands. "Other folktales" include subgenres like novelle or romantic tales, which tend to have less magic than straight-up fairy tales and are thought of as a reflection of daily life with witty commentary (tale types in this arena include many of the stories that show up in *The Canterbury Tales*, for example, with realistic stock characters like peasants and priests who outwit and/or cuckold each other). American folklorist Stith Thompson published an updated version in 1928 (which was also translated into English, as Aarne's index was published in German). Thompson's version took into account more of these regional versions and corrected some inconsistencies. However, as feminist scholars have noted, the tale type index still contained many erasures of female agency, which the Uther revision of 2004 finally addressed (see Lundell).

So, why are we folklore scholars so into tale types? They allow us to study the international transmission of folktales and fairy tales. You can bet your Bettelheim that "Cinderella" isn't called "Cinderella" in every culture where it's told, so it's useful to have a way to keep track of the types as they travel through different linguistic and cultural regions. Because folklorists document the interplay of tradition and variation, having a starting point for comparison – the type – is extremely useful.

Is the type a perfect concept? Does it exist independently of human observation? Ehhh not so much. Francisco Vaz da Silva takes folklorists to task for having "fallen into the habit of taking arbitrarily defined types for things out there and… thinking accordingly" (115). This can lead to problems if we assume that there are, in fact, ideal/prior versions of tale types that extant versions *should* live up to, and that the versions in circulation are faulty or degraded if they don't. In reality, types are quite fluid, so it's helpful to keep that in mind even as we use tools like the type index to help with our research.

If you want to work with tale types, you have to get your hands on the updated tale type index, the 2004 one released by Hans-Jörg Uther. A Norwegian university site has a good breakdown of many of the tale type numbers,[1] including an explanation of what was changed in the most recent version of the index.[2] Trust me, it's a real folklore pet peeve when people use AT numbers instead of ATU numbers… the ATU index has been out for over a decade, people! Get your hands on it, or get to a library that has it!

Most folklorists can rattle off at least half a dozen tale type numbers, which makes for a fun party trick if nothing else. At any rate, the concept of the type has been around for almost a century (longer if you trace out its history in philological writings of the 19th century), and it's central to the way folklorists study narrative.

References:

Lundell, Torborg. "Folktale Heroines and the Type and Motif." *Folklore* vol. 94, no. 2, 1983, pp. 240-246.

Thompson, Stith. *The Folktale*. University of California Press, 1977 [1946].

Vaz da Silva, Francisco. *Metamorphosis: The Dynamics of Symbolism in European Fairy Tales*. Peter Lang, 2002.

FIXED-PHRASE VS. FREE-PHRASE

Ever heard a tongue-twister? Then you've heard fixed-phrase folklore before. Here's what it means in terms of other verbal arts genres.

In folklore studies, we consider a large swath of folklore to be verbal arts, or transmitted in/through language and sound. Since we're attuned not only to text and context but also texture, we ask: what makes verbal folklore unique in terms of its linguistic patterns? How are words arranged in ways that contribute to the meaning?

Thus, we distinguish between fixed-phrase and free-phrase folklore.

Fixed-phrase folklore is usually repeated word-for-word, without variation on that level. Examples include folk speech items (where the word itself is the item of folklore, like "hella") as well as proverbs. Nursery rhymes and folk songs might also fit in this category, since "Rock a bye baby" usually stays the same, unless it's a parody. And of course there are tongue twisters, a minor verbal genre in which the challenge (and hilarity) comes from tricky verbal sequences that are progressively more difficult to pronounce quickly and sequentially. If you've studied other languages, you may have had an inventive teacher give you tongue twisters in that language, as it's a great way to practice the different sounds and syllables. One example (in English, anyway) is "How much wood would a woodchuck chuck if a woodchuck could chuck wood?" And some tongue twisters are regarded as a "catch" genre too, where slipping up could mean uttering a curse word by accident (for instance: "I slit a sheet, a sheet I slit; Upon a slitted sheet I sit"). These are all fixed-phrase because their wording more or less stays the same over time, though innovations happen too, and jokes may begin with one of these classic phrases and then mutate into something else.

Free-phrase folklore can be expressed in any kind of language and still be coherent. If I'm telling a folktale, specifically a fairy tale, I can use a lot of different words to convey the plot. There are probably going to be some consistencies across tellings (such as opening and closing formulas like "Once upon a time" and "They lived happily ever after"), but as far as the rest of the narrative, I can describe things the way I want to. I may or may not go into Cinderella's hair color, for example (traditional versions of the tale don't always specify; it's only thanks to Disney that we have a concrete visual of how Cinderella looks and what her ball gown looks like; in contrast, Snow White's physical description it built into the narrative itself, and often described in a fixed-phrase kind of way, e.g., "The queen wished for a child as white as snow, as red as blood, and as black as ebony" or some variation thereon). It's similar with jokes; sometimes the punchline requires precise phrasing, but mostly you can tell a narrative joke in any fashion you want. Once the priest and rabbi walk into the bar, any number of shenanigans can ensue!

We utilize this distinction to help us track tradition and variation at work. If a proverb, for example, has been mostly fixed-phrase in the past, but suddenly leaps into free-phrase expression? That's something we'd want to study. Different languages utilize poetic devices differently, so we might find each genre lining up differently with fixed- vs. free-phrase patterns.

Because I spent so long describing variation as an essential component of identifying folklore, I do want to clarify that fixed-phrase folklore still counts as folklore. Often, there's still variation going on but it's more subtle. It may not be happening so much as the textural level, the wording itself, but rather, in how the text is being used (as in, its function). I like the example of the proverb, "A rolling stone gathers no moss." This one is pretty fixed-phrase; I don't tend to hear variations such as (and this is just me making things up), "A rolling rock gathers no moss" or "Stones in motion don't attract algae" or whatever. I think where the variation comes in with this text is in the meaning and the function: what does the moss represent? Is the moss a good thing or a bad thing? I might utter this proverb approvingly to a friend who just got out of a bad relationship and is enjoying the single life, implying that moss = attachments that weigh you down. Alternately, if the same free-wheeling friend seemed ambivalent about enjoying the single life but also expressed a desire to settle down and start a family, I might use that proverb to say that moss = the good kind of attachments, the kind you grow when you decide to prioritize those things. Same proverb, different potential meanings.

Describing verbal folklore genres in terms of their

linguistic patterns helps us classify folklore in terms of its content, structure, and style. It's rarely an ironclad way to go (because language, folklore, and culture are slippery like that), but it gives us a useful place to start.

THE EPIC LAWS OF FOLK NARRATIVE

One of the conferences I attend yearly to get my fairy tale and fantasy fix is ICFA, the International Conference on the Fantastic in the Arts. In my conference recap of ICFA 38: Fantastic Epics,[1] I mentioned that I was on a panel about the intersections of fairy tales and epics. While defining epic is its own – dare I say – epic task, I thought I'd bring a little something else to the table: Axel Olrik's epic laws of folk narrative.

I apparently have a thing for dead Danish folklorists. Axel Olrik is one of these people.

Olrik (1864-1917) was a pioneering figure in international folkloristics, earning him a spot in Alan Dundes's edited volume of that title. Among other things, Olrik was instrumental in founding the Folklore Fellows, an international scholarly society that helped grow the academic discipline of folkloristics, and is still in existence today. Olrik studied with Svend Grundtvig, a major Danish ballad scholar, and Norwegian Moltke Moe (who collaborated on a classic folktale collection).

As Dundes summarizes Olrik's contributions:

> One of Olrik's apparent goals was to determine whether there were characteristics of what he called "Sage," an inclusive term by which he meant myth, folktale, legend, and folksong that could help to distinguish folklore from written literature. He suggested that as a given oral narrative enters written domain, it tends to lose its distinctive character as reflected in various epic laws. Regardless of whether this is so and also of whether Olrik's laws apply to the folklore of non-European cultures, there can be no question that his effort to articulate laws or principles of folk narrative constitutes a landmark in international folkloristics. (86)

So what are these epic laws? I'll turn now to Olrik's own words:

> In popular narrative, storytellers have a tendency to observe certain practices in composition and style that are generally common to large areas and different categories of narratives, including most of the European narrative tradition. The regularity with which these practices appear make it possible for us to regard them as "epic laws" of oral narrative composition. (41)

When we study folk narrative, we tend to break it into distinct genres, based upon stylistic qualities, relationship to reality/belief, and so on. What Olrik's saying is that what matters more than genre boundaries is that it's verbal folklore, orally transmitted, since there are narrative conventions that performers tend to follow in order to aid with cohesion, audience memory, and so on. Olrik ties the epic laws to the need for clarity of narrative when a narrative is being transmitted orally, with all the constraints that entails.

Without further ado, here are the epic laws:

- The Law of Two to a Scene: in most folk narratives, we'll see two characters at a time interacting, unless a third is briefly introduced to play a subordinate role.
- The Law of Concentration on a Leading Character: Olrik describes this as how "The narrative always arranges itself around a main character. It includes what concerns him and disregards everything else" (49).
- The Law of Contrast: as Olrik puts it, "When two characters appear at the same time, the narrative will establish a contrast in character between them, often also a contrast in action. The contrasts between good and evil, poor and rich, big and small, young and old, etc., are very common" (50).
- The Law of Twins: "When two characters appear in the same role, they are both depicted as being weaker than a single character" (51).
- The Law of Three: "The narrative has a preference for the number three in characters, in objects, and in successive episodes" (52). We see this magnified as things coming in multiples of three, too, such as a

dragon that has siblings with nine and twelve heads.

- The Law of Final Stress: "When several narrative elements are set alongside each other, emphasis is placed on the last in the sequence: the youngest of three brothers, the last of three attempts, etc. The epically important character is normally in the 'position of final stress.' On the other hand, the most impressive character is placed first: the eldest of several brothers, the mightiest of several gods, and the like. This is designated as 'initial stress' and does not concern narrative research" (52). I followed the footnote to figure out what Olrik meant here, and it's not entirely clear, as this publication was prepared from his lecture notes. My guess is that he was hinting that initial stress is more a thing in religious or written literature than oral tradition.
- The Law of Opening: "In the beginning of the narrative, one moves (1) from the individual to the multiple, (2) from calm to excitement, and (3) from the everyday to the unusual" (55).
- The Law of Closing: "The account normally ends after the decisive event, but preferably not so suddenly that the audience is startled; the atmosphere must have time to calm down and to disappear gradually from the main character and the main episodes. A short, concluding story serves this purpose, e.g., (1) the later fate of the main character, particularly in such a way that one follows him through to a lasting, often lingering or resting state; (2) the influence of the fate of the main character on others, e.g., that his mother or his

> betrothed dies from grief; (3) the fate of the subordinate characters, e.g., the punishment of the villain in the account; (4) visible memories of the event, such as the reappearance of the protagonist as a ghost" (55-56).

There are also a number of epic laws that aren't as pithy as the ones summarized above; these include repetition through progressive assent (each fight the hero must win is more difficult than the last), the unity of the plot (how a plot aspires to a single event and excludes extraneous details that don't contribute to this), and the single-strandedness of plot (how folk narrative plots don't generally break away to return to something that had already happened, unless it's super relevant to the plot moving forward). There's more about unity of plot vs. ideal epic unity of plot, but I won't go into that here.

Stylistically, Olrik also describes the importance of what he calls tableaux scenes:

> In these scenes, the actors draw near to each other: the hero and his horse; the hero and the monster; Thor pulls the World Serpent up to the edge of the boat; the valiant warriors die so near to their king that even in death they protect him; Siegmund carries his dead son himself.
>
> These sculptured situations are based more on fantasy than on reality; the hero's sword is scorched by the dragon's breath; the maiden, standing on the back of a bull or snake, surveys the scene; from her own breasts the banished queen squeezes milk into the beaks of a swan and a crane. (quoted in Dundes, 94)

Further, these tableaux scenes exist because, according to Olrik, they "possess the singular power of being able to etch themselves into one's memory" (quoted in Dundes, 95).

And that's what this is all about: discerning where the stylistic and structural qualities of folk narrative converge to make art so memorable that it persists in oral (and sometimes written) tradition. Some of the epic laws of folk narrative get weighted differently, or even discarded, in certain genres of folklore, but they provide an excellent starting point for comparative research.

References:

Dundes, Alan, editor. *International Folkloristics: Classic Contributions by the Founders of Folklore*. Rowman & Littlefield Publishers Inc., 1999.

Olrik, Axel. *Principles for Oral Narrative Research*. Translated by Kirsten Wolf and Jody Jensen. Indiana University Press, 1992 [1921].

BIG CATEGORIES OF FOLKLORE

WHAT IS A "BIG CATEGORY OF FOLKLORE"?

Well, lots of words that would make more sense are already taken. When someone says "forms of folklore" there's already a connotation that maybe we're talking about the forms that folklore takes, like specific genres (more on those in the next section!), or form as a stylistic trait that corresponds more to texture. We can't say "types of folklore" because again, that sounds very genre-y, and additionally, we have the concept of tale type to compete for that use of type.

Folklorists already have to deal with the fact that the word "function" has two very distinct meanings: it can mean the role/purpose/ "why" of folklore OR the specific event in a folktale/fairy-tale that advances the plot in Vladimir Propp's structural analysis of Russian tales, explained in his classic book *Morphology of the Folktale*. So I'm doing my best to avoid this sort of accidental reuse of words!

What we'll see in this section is the general shape that many folklore genres have in common. I almost called them "incarnations of folklore" but that was a little too reminiscent of my awkward teenage years reading Piers Anthony. Though – stay with me a moment – I do think there's something to the notion that a given culture's worldview (a.k.a. the dominant paradigm, belief system, etc. of a group) finds expressions, or, one might say *incarnations*, in a variety of folklore genres, which is also something we discuss under the not-quite-genre-but-close-enough concept of folk ideas, or clearly folkloric ideas/values/stuff that doesn't have a happy relationship with the genre sorting hat and tends to pop up in multiple genres. All of which is to say, I think the big ideas and themes that a culture is interested in will resurface in multiple arenas, from pop culture to literature to folklore, and thus I think it's interesting to consider that maybe folklore manifests whatever a culture is concerned with, like an idea taking a concrete form. Hence the incarnation metaphor that I don't ultimately use very often in this book, because I'm still chewing on it.

Anyway, this notion of Big Chunks O' Folklore would then get sorted into genres and subgenres, the idea being that lots of traditional culture is multifaceted and can take many shapes, but there are some types of shapes that have traits in common, along with the genres that get sorted under them. Using this metaphor, you might imagine that verbal folklore tends to be circular, so the genres that fall under it (like fairy tales, legends, proverbs, and so on) all have the traits of circles (some are ovals, ellipses, etc.). In turn, we could envision customary folklore as a rectangular prism (so customs and folk dances and so on would be a variety of squares, rectangles, and trapezoids) while material culture might be triangles (with body art, foodways, and so on as a variety of equilateral, scalene, etc. triangles). I arbitrarily chose which shape pairs with which large category of folklore (is there anything circular about verbal folklore? Maybe for shaggy dog stories!) but hopefully it illustrates the point.

Alternately, you might envision each of these big categories as an umbrella or a giant tree that casts a lot of shade: the verbal folklore tree or umbrella has within its purview jokes, fairy tales, legends, and so on through the list.

Remember, however, from the introduction that everything we consider folklore has some core stuff in common: no matter what shape it takes, story or meme or folk medicine, it's informally transmitted traditional culture. It's not locked up in a textbook or behind a paywall, it's a living tradition curated by and for the people who encounter it. So while I enjoy my weird metaphors of geometrical shapes and umbrellas and such, it's important to keep in mind that on the surface, two folklore texts might look *extremely* different from one another, enough that you're perhaps thinking, "Um, WTF, why do my grandma's quilts and this Biden meme both count as folklore?" It's because of how they're transmitted through informal rather than institutional means, no matter which shape they take at the other end of the process. It's because we can document that both tradition and variation are at work: look, there are a bunch of Biden memes, demonstrating the stable thread of tradition even as there are lots of variations on the imagery and messages therein.

So, read on to learn more about what I consider the three main big categories of folklore: verbal folklore, customary folklore, and material culture.

VERBAL FOLKLORE

IF YOU'VE HEARD or used slang, or encountered an urban legend, then you, my friend, have been exposed to verbal folklore! Perhaps you've even performed it!!!

In folklore studies we tend to classify texts by genre, meaning that we group similar items of folklore together and slap a label on them. However, we also talk about categories of folklore in broad ways related to the medium in which they're transmitted, and that's what this section of *Folklore 101* covers.

One of the easiest ways to divide up the major categories of folklore is to sort them into things people say, things people do, and things people make. Some scholars add things people believe to this list, though I usually group it under things people do.

The first of these, things people say, is considered in more scholarly language to be verbal folklore. Verbal folklore – also called verbal arts or oral folklore – encompasses the realm of folklore transmitted in language.

Here's how Lynne McNeill characterizes it in *Folklore Rules*:

> The category of things we say encompasses all folklore that comes out of our mouths or through our fingertips and onto a piece of paper or a screen. That means jokes, slang, proverbs, riddles, mnemonic devices, rhymes, songs, oaths, toasts, greetings, leave-takings – basically tons and tons of forms of folklore – but the most famous, the most well-known, the most studied forms of verbal folklore are stories. (38)

Jan Brunvand characterizes this category of folklore as such:

> Oral folklore, the type most commonly studied until fairly recently in the United States, may be conveniently arranged and listed from the simplest to the most complex varieties. At the level of the individual word is *folk speech*, including dialect and naming. Traditional phrases and sentences make up the area of folk *proverbs* and *proverbial sayings*, while traditional questions are folk *riddles*. Next are folk *rhymes* and other traditional poetry, then folk *narratives* of all kinds, and finally folk *songs* and folk *ballads* with their music. (11, italics in original)

Because most verbal folklore genres are expressed in language, we use a lot of concepts from linguistics and literary analysis to study them. So we might talk about whether certain texts are fixed-phrase or free-phrase, what sorts of motifs and themes they contain, and so on. Most folk narratives fall under verbal folklore (though there are certainly narratives expressed in other forms) so we tend to associate narrative analysis with verbal folklore too. In terms of their texture, it's often useful to look at the stylistic qualities of verbal folklore using the same concepts we'd use to analyze poetry: alliteration, consonance, assonance, rhyme, meter/rhythm, and so on. These concepts, too, vary by language and culture.

As you'll see in the genres section, I've already written about some verbal folklore genres to highlight their unique and shared traits. Those include: folk speech, proverb, Wellerism, folk metaphor & folk simile, dite, ballad, folk song (& folk music sometimes), joke, joke cycles, personal narrative, folktale, fairy tale, legend, and myth. Folk song and folk music are occasionally edge cases; how carefully should we differentiate between the version of a lullaby with words (thus, verbal folklore) and the version that's just hummed (still a human voice doing things, but no words to analyze)?

Since I work so much with narrative, I guess it's not a surprise that I've blogged about a ton of verbal folklore topics already. When it comes down to it, I've been a language and story nerd for most of my life.

Again, the key determining factor in whether something counts as folklore is how it's transmitted: whether it's conveyed through official/institutional cultural channels, or unofficial (a.k.a. "folk") ones. Not all language is folklore, but when folklore is conveyed in/of language, we consider it to be verbal folklore.

References:

Brunvand, Jan Harold. *The Study of American Folklore: An Introduction*. Fourth edition. W. W. Norton & Company, 1998 [1968, 1978, 1986].

McNeill, Lynne S. *Folklore Rules: A Fun, Quick, and Useful Introduction to the Field of Academic Folklore Studies*. Utah State University Press, 2013.

CUSTOMARY FOLKLORE

WHEN FOLKLORE CROSSES into the realm of religion, ritual, festival, and holiday, we consider it customary folklore: cultural materials people learn traditionally.

In the last chapter, I defined verbal folklore as all the various types of folklore that are expressed orally / aurally / linguistically. Here, I'll describe customary folklore, which is based more in the realm of actions and beliefs.

There is, of course, some debate as to where these broad categories begin and end. I lump traditional behaviors and beliefs into the same category, while Lynne McNeill considers them separately in her book *Folklore Rules*. Here's her take on both areas:

> When it comes to things we do, we're entering an incredibly broad area of folklore studies. Customs (like holiday traditions), gestures (like a thumbs-up or flipping someone off), parties (like costume parties or tea

> parties), rituals (like fraternity or sorority initiations, or bar mitzvahs), celebrations (like sixteenth or twenty-first birthday parties), dances (like the two-step, the "Macarena," the electric slide, the chicken dance), games (like kick the can, tag, capture the flag, and four-square)...these are all things we do, and since many of them exist in forms that we learn informally, from our experiences in regular, everyday life, they fall under the purview of folklore. The quality these things all share in common, of course, is that they require some kind of action – some type of body movement or physical participation in the tradition. (44)
>
> [T]he category of things we believe overlaps with all the other forms of folklore quite regularly. As a discrete form of folklore, however, the phrase "folk belief" is commonly understood to refer to superstitions, legends, and beliefs about the supernatural. Now, there's one very important thing to note at the outset of any discussion about folk belief, and that is that *folklore can be true.* It certainly isn't always true, despite often being believed, but the classification of something as folklore does not mean that it's specifically not true. (56, italics in original)

Again, my take is that it's easier to lump in belief with behavior, though there are reasons to do it otherwise. I tend to view belief as difficult to articulate unless there's an actionable component to it; this is part of why folk ideas and worldview are so tough to isolate and study.

Jan Brunvand talks about customary folklore as follows: "Customary folklore, which often involves both verbal and nonverbal elements, includes folk *beliefs* and *superstitions*, folk *customs* and *festivals*, folk *dances* and *dramas*, traditional *gestures*, and folk *games*" (11).

As has been observed, much of folklore is already customary in nature, at least in terms of its transmission. Even when we're talking about a pretty straight-up verbal genre of folklore, like a narrative, in folkloric contexts the active bearers of that narrative would likely have learned how to be a good storyteller through observation, not necessarily through reading a book or taking a college course on the subject.

But the experience or performance of customary folklore is especially, well, experiential. This relates to McNeill's observation:

> Thus, the modes of transmission for this kind of folklore are largely observational. Unlike a legend, which can be e-mailed as easily as told in person, it's not so easy to e-mail someone a Thanksgiving dinner celebration. Maybe you could e-mail someone an aspect of the custom, like a photo of the turkey or a copy of the toast someone gave, but not the whole experience. (44)

Brunvand echoes McNeill's emphasis on the experiential aspect of customary folklore, noting:

> Placing a folksinger's lyrics in one category, his or her guitar-playing style and melody in another, and the call and figures of a dance done to the same song in a third is

> not intended to lead to fragmentation of either the tradition involved or the study of it...Without an awareness of these elements of a traditional performance, there would be a tendency simply to tape-record 'the song' without capturing its context or nonverbal nuances. (11)

So, we're aiming for as much holistic analysis as possible, aided by these categories rather than constrained by them.

This is a major area where religion and folklore intersect, too: the spaces where beliefs and behaviors unite the human and divine or supernatural worlds. As always, our mission as folklorists is to document and analyze without necessarily judging. That said, I personally move through the world as a mostly agnostic/atheist type of person, yearning for the empirical while being open-minded about things I don't understand yet.

Examples of customary folklore genres that I cover in subsequent chapters include: superstition and folk belief, ritual, rite of passage, ostension, holiday, folk dance, folk music (and folk songs), folk religion/vernacular religion, and folk medicine. I'm also considering folk ideas close enough to lump in here.

There are always more, but those are some of the major ones I've written about. And, since I like giving people food for thought: what sorts of customary folklore do you engage in?

References:

Brunvand, Jan Harold. *The Study of American Folklore: An Introduction*. Fourth edition. W. W. Norton & Company, 1998 [1968, 1978, 1986].

McNeill, Lynne S. *Folklore Rules: A Fun, Quick, and Useful Introduction to the Field of Academic Folklore Studies*. Utah State University Press, 2013.

MATERIAL CULTURE

I'M A NARRATIVE SCHOLAR, so I play in the verbal folklore sandbox a lot. But folklore also encompasses customs and beliefs and physical items, the latter of which I'll cover here. My plan is to define material culture, describe some of the strategies we use to study it from a folkloristic perspective, and give some examples. It's such a huge topic that there's no way this post can be exhaustive, but here goes!

Material culture is, to put it glibly, culture made material. In the realm of folklore – or informally transmitted traditional culture – we consider material culture to be the physical manifestation of folklore. The other stuff we study is usually expressed verbally or in behavior/belief (as covered in previous chapters) whereas material culture has a physical presence in the world but is still folkloric in nature (whereas a physical anthropologist or archaeologist might study other types of objects or artifacts that wouldn't necessarily interest folklorists).

We distinguish between objects created out of nature, and those created out of culture (often called assemblage). The clay a potter digs from the earth comes straight from nature, whereas a quilter using scraps of fabric is constructing her art from premade cultural materials. Other types of material culture might be a blend, as when people make dioramas using both leaves and sticks as well as glue and cardboard.

Lynne McNeill writes:

> When most people think of folk objects (often referred to as "material culture" by folklorists), they usually think of handmade goods: furniture, tools, clothing, quilts, decorative cross-stitching, and the like. Handcrafts are, indeed, one of the most studied forms of material culture. For a long period of history, if you wanted something you had to make it; one result of this is that the qualities of folklore (variation and tradition) were easily found in many of the objects that people had in their homes – they had learned the general form and style of furniture from those around them (tradition), and through varied levels of ability and creativity they'd add their own individual touches (variation). (51)

Jan Brunvand's definition of the area is much briefer: "Material folk traditions include folk architecture, crafts, arts, costumes, and food" (11).

Brunvand's description focuses more on items that originate in folkloric ways, whereas the items McNeill discusses have a bit more leeway in terms of origin. McNeill reminds us that "mass-produced objects become folk objects when they are turned into something else...[and] when they are used in an unexpected, traditional way" (52). In other words, patterns of use can help transform a commercial object (like a garden gnome or Barbie doll) into something folklorists are interested in studying.

In contrast to verbal folklore, which is uttered by its performer, material culture can be studied in three contexts that are unique to it:

- Creation
- Communication
- Consumption

What's really fascinating here is that unlike with the process of narrating a joke or carrying out a superstition, we *can* observe the context of creating material culture. I can't peek inside a narrator's brain when they're telling a joke or a story, but I can watch a sculptor's hands, or a make-up artist's brushes, at work. I can observe and ask questions about the specific techniques and tools involved, which is super cool.

In addition to the context of creation, we want to ask questions about the context of communication, which is also distinct from verbal and customary folklore in a few key ways. One of the main concepts we use to study folklore is that of function or how folklore always communicates or accomplishes something in the world. If you record a narrative from a narrator, it becomes words on a page or a voice on an audio recording, and it communicates outside of its normal performance context. But if you take a quilt or friendship bracelet away from its maker, *that's already how it was intended to function for the most part*. Material culture *already* speaks apart from its makers. And that is freakin' cool (and a point I am not likely to forget, given that one of my dissertation advisors, Dr. Pravina Shukla, emphasized it during my PhD qualifying exams).

Finally, material culture is consumed in noteworthy ways. When it comes to food, yes, the object is literally consumed. But other material culture texts get used and displayed in ways that are unique because they occupy the physical realm. The concept of texture applies literally in some cases; we're not just talking about the stylistic qualities of a verbal arts genre like a proverb but about the texture of a pot, a basket, a loaf of bread, a piece of jewelry. If you've got any fine arts background, this is the time to bust it out, and describe the item's use of color, contrast, shape, dynamism, line, and so on.

My material culture chapters in the next section cover the following genres: body art, foodways, folk art, and the instruments associated with music. Vernacular architecture – how people house themselves in non/pre-industrial settings – is also a big topic, but it's never one that's resonated with me so um, go read something by Henry Glassie since he's written a few classics on the topic?

Material culture weaves in and out of verbal and customary folklore too; rites of passage often have elaborate costumes and foods associated with them, and folk medicine usually has a physical component to it. Getting a handle on how specifically we study material culture is thus an important step in understanding folklore more generally.

References:

Brunvand, Jan Harold. *The Study of American Folklore: An Intro-*

duction. Fourth edition. W. W. Norton & Company, 1998 [1968, 1978, 1986].

McNeill, Lynne S. *Folklore Rules: A Fun, Quick, and Useful Introduction to the Field of Academic Folklore Studies*. Utah State University Press, 2013.

FOLKLORE GENRES

GENRES INTRO & THE FOUR-PART RUBRIC

By now you know that genres are categories or forms of folklore that display loads of similarities. So you can hold up a bunch of fairy tales or quilts alongside other examples from that genre, and see both where they differ from one another (variation!) and where their traits converge (tradition!). Sometimes you'll see persistent motifs and/or themes across genres, which is one of the things I do in my research when I study the depiction of sex and sexuality in both fairy tales and urban legends, for instance (spoiler: both genres are super judgey about women who've had more than one partner).

This section takes you on a tour of many of the major folklore genres that have been studied by academic folklorists in the West. Why the cagey phrasing? Well, over the past few centuries of my discipline's history, scholars have tended to prioritize both what they know and what they find to be pleasingly exotic. So a lot of folklore scholarship has focused on Ye Olden Times in European and American cultures (the familiar) as well as on What Those People Over There Who Don't Look Like Us Do (the unfamiliar, which risks having a bunch of ethnocentric assumptions baked into the scholarship). We're kinda-sorta doing better now, thanks to the reflexive turn in folklore studies and anthropology in the 1980s and 1990s, as well as ideas ranging from post-colonialism to Critical Race Theory helping inform our thinking.

Many of my genre examples are from American cultures because that's what my undergraduate and graduate studies tended to focus on, but I'm also going to caveat this statement: "American" has become something of a catchall term for *white* Americans, and that's worth noting. As my colleague Rachel González-Martin asserts: "*American* is a deracialized social descriptor akin to *mainstream* or *normal*; it has a silent racial subtext but can still be argued to be inclusive in mixed company. The use of such terms manifests an invisible Center" (24, italics in original). She suggests instead the use of the term USAmerican to note the historic centering of Anglo-descended and/or white communities in folklore studies, and so while I use the term "American folklore" uncritically in these chapters, some of which were written up to 5 years ago, I do want to note that USAmerican is a more accurate way to filter this knowledge.

Mostly, I want to be clear that these genres aren't necessarily universally important ones. These aren't "THE" folklore genres. They're just the ones I learned in undergrad and grad school. And while most cultures will likely have folk speech, and folk narrative, and ritual, and body art, just how those genres look and feel and take on meaning may look vastly different across time and space. Some things tend to be universal across human cultures – everyone has some notion of family, everyone has language and stories, everyone needs to eat food – but the specifics of how those things manifest are quite variable. So I don't want anyone reading these chapters to come away thinking that you've now mastered all folklore genres (kinda icky phrasing in and of itself, eh?) and are good to go. The beauty of folklore is in its inherent variability, so there'll always be stuff that's new in general, or new to you.

The way I organized this section is the way I learned about folklore under Alan Dundes. We learn first about verbal folklore, then customary folklore, then material culture. In the verbal folklore segment, we start with short verbal genres that might be more relatable, such as folk speech (a.k.a. slang or dialect) and proverbs, and then we move on to folk narrative genres. Those are my specialty so I spend a lot of time on them (sorry/not sorry). Not every genre fits that neat "big categories of folklore" division, such as folk medicine, which has both customary and physical components to it, but this is meant as a rough guide, not the ultimate definitive genre breakdown. Like I mentioned above, the terrain of folklore is constantly shifting because that's just what folklore *does*. Besides, we still need stuff to argue over at conferences!

There are other ways to approach folklore genres, of course. While I was a grad student at Indiana University, I TAed for Dr. Nicole Kousaleos, whose feminist approach to teaching taught me tons. She structured her Folklore 101 class to follow the life cycle: we learned about birth rituals and rites of passage, and then about children's folklore, and then about urban legends that are important to teenagers, and so on. Other folklorists look at genres through the lens of folk group or region. Still others use performance as a way to think about genre. So there are multiple ways to go about this, I'm just choosing the one that I'm most familiar with and that resonates the most with me.

And, of course, genre categories are a scholarly construct in some ways, and are permeable in others. I mean, if you stand around with friends telling jokes and someone utters a proverb instead, everyone will be confused, because there's an insider or native understanding of which genre was supposed to come into play right then. But very few people use the same scholarly language we do in their daily lives, which imbues our genre labels with a bit of artificiality. Sometimes the boundaries between adjacent boundaries blur: for instance, try to disentangle fake news and conspiracy theory from urban legend and rumor these days, and let me know if you get anywhere!

So again, please understand that the genres that follow are scholarly categories, an attempt to pin a living tradition to a board in order to better understand it. Not perfect, but what we've got to work with.

Finally, I want to give you a paradigm I've been using for the last few years in my college classes in order to help students dig into individual genres: the four-part rubric. This is covered somewhat in the above sections (especially functions and text, texture, and context) so the material repeats a bit if you've been closely reading everything up through this point, but I'll also try to reframe the material in a way that's unique and useful.

The four-part rubric is a way of breaking down folklore genres into their individual components: content, context, form, and function. Content is what the thing is or what's in the thing, context is who/when/where the thing is transmitted, form is how the thing is transmitted and what shape it takes, and function is why the thing is transmitted or what its overall purpose is.

If you're familiar with the journalist's 5 questions to approach a topic (who, what, where, when, why, and how), these also map pretty well onto the four-part rubric. Content is the what: to draw on one of my favorite genres, fairy tales, the content is what's in the story and what the story is about (princesses, magic rings, and so on; so in verbal genres, content often relates to motif and theme). Content is what you're asking about if your friend just saw a movie and you ask, "Oh, what's it about?" In narrative genres, content often relates to plot, character, and setting. Please note, however, that the story or text's setting still counts as something *inside* the story; when I'm talking about setting, I am not talking about the context, or where the story might have been told, performed, or recorded. Context is everything outside or surrounding the story, while content is everything inside the story (apologies for lingering here; this is a point that not everyone grasps at first and I've marked many a paper that accidentally conflated content and context).

Context is the who, where, and when of the thing. If the thing is a story, then context is who is performing it (teller), to whom (audience), where (both local and global), and when (both time of the day and time period). The context when the Grimms were collecting fairy tales (early 1800s not-yet-unified-Germany) looks a lot different than the context when French writers like Charles Perrault and Madame d'Aulnoy were writing their fairy tales (under the authoritarian reign of Louis XIV in France, and specifically while the authors hung out in salons with their peers). When thinking about context, we ask questions like which stories (or rituals, or recipes, or whatever) are appropriate in a given time of day or season, and whether it's okay to have kids in the audience or not. We want to know what day and month and year this is taking place in, as well as in which country and region, and heck, whether it's an urban or rural settings. Paying attention to context means paying attention to loads of detail that can inform how the folklore is being shaped and transmitted in that moment.

This leads us to form, or the how of the thing. I tend to use form and structure almost synonymously, since "form" can be vague at times, and structure clearly indicates that we're talking about how something is put together. But if we're going to talk about form as structure, we can't neglect style, or the artistic sense of how something is put together (this is congruent with texture, discussed in the earlier chapter about text, texture, and context). For verbal genres, form also includes language: how is the tale being told? Are we hearing alliteration, rhyme, and other poetic devices? (this is the chance to whip out any terms you recall from English literature classes!) In the chapter on fixed-phrase vs. free-phrase genres, the focus was largely on form: how, linguistically, are these proverbs and such being conveyed? When do minute changes to the language matter? In turn, for genres that are more visual (such as quilting), form is about pattern, repetition, contrast, and use of color (this is where those of you with some art training can really put your vocabulary to use!). Whether we're talking verbal or visual genres, though, form remains an investigation of how something is put together, structured, made to convey meaning using recognizable (and traditional, since this is folklore) patterns.

Finally, function. It got its own chapter so I'll be brief here. In terms of the journalistic questions, function corresponds to why. Why are these tales told? Why are these customs performed? Why are these foods consumed? Since folklore isn't mandated the same way that legal and educational institutional cultures are, folklore doesn't stick around unless it serves some kind of purpose, and function addresses that purpose. Sometimes people are really good at articulating the function of the folklore they're involved in, and sometimes not. Honestly, I think that culture operates on levels that are both conscious and unconscious/subconscious, so it makes sense that we're at best only partially aware of the registers of culture that compose our daily lives. I mean, have you ever sat someone down and asked them to explain every single one of their values and beliefs? It's not easy to do on the fly. Our belief systems overlap and sometimes conflict, and we can't always trace where each and every belief comes from or how deeply it's ingrained in us. Because culture is so complicated, there are a lot of potential "whys" floating around, and hence attempting to address function means taking into account the other parts of the four-part rubric: content, context, and form. Context can drive new demands in people's lives, shaping the content and form of the folklore, which we can hopefully study in order to understand function and the whole picture in more nuanced ways than ever.

Obviously, the four parts of the four-part rubric aren't entirely discrete and separate from one another. A classic example from fairy tales is how context influences content: fairy tales from France often feature fairies and fairy godmothers as the main magic helper figures, while fairy tales from Germany have a mix of witches, sorceresses, and dead parental figures helping out. One hypothesis about the content of European fairy tales brings in their function: maybe the reason we have so many step-families in European fairy tales is because maternal mortality rates were high and famines were common when the genre was first germinated in the 16th and 17th centuries, so you found a lot of blended families because it reflected people's social reality, and it also gave people hopeful stories about how things would turn out all right.

Remember, the four-part rubric is a tool to help you understand genres better. Line up a bunch of texts from a genre – say, a bunch of fairy tales, or a bunch of urban legends – and you'll start to find similarities among their content, context, form, and function. Those similarities show you where tradition is happening, while the differences are works of variation. Sometimes you think a text belongs to a genre when in fact it's got so many outliers in terms of its content, context, form, and function that you have to reconsider its genre classification. On the flip side, studying a text in isolation doesn't always give you enough information to determine its function, though you could always get some use out of doing a lit-crit-style deep dive into a single text and analyzing its form and artistry, or connecting it to its teller/maker/performer's life story and cultural context. Quick example of a text in isolation: Charles Perrault's version of "Little Red Riding Hood" has the wolf eat the girl in the end, and she does *not* get rescued and revived... so if this were the only instance of a fairy tale I'd read, I might erroneously assume that most fairy tales had unhappy endings! Assembling multiple texts from a genre and running them through the four-part rubric is almost always a good starting point for understanding that genre better, so I hope it is a useful tool for you in your own work!

References:

González-Martin, Rachel. "White Traditioning and Bruja Epistemologies: Rebuilding the House of USAmerican Folklore Studies." *Theorizing Folklore from the Margins: Critical and Ethical Approaches*, edited by Solimar Otero and Mintzi Auanda Martínez-Rivera, Indiana University Press, 2021, 22-41.

FOLK SPEECH

Hey. Sup. Ciao. What do all these greetings have in common? They're informal traditional usages of language, a.k.a. folk speech.

Folklorist Jan Brunvand defines folk speech as "the traditional word, expression, usage, or name that is current in a folk group or in a particular region" (73). Examples range from dialect like "y'all" in the American south to what you call the fizzy sugary stuff that comes in cans, which Americans argue about as being soda vs. pop vs. coke.

Folk speech texts are often brief, as short as one word. But getting too hung up on texts isn't a good idea here; since we're talking about the study of language, we're not simply scouting for words that seem unique or quaint. We're also looking for syntax and grammar that display variation. For instance, in California we say "the" before naming a highway or interstate: "I'm going to take the 5 down to SoCal." But since moving to Indiana, I've noticed that people exclude the "the," such as:

"Ugh, it's rush hour, I'm not getting on 465 even if my life depends on it."

The thing I love about folk speech is that we're all active bearers of it. We all use slang, and we all speak in dialect to some degree. This is why when I assign folklore collections to my students, I'm surprised when there's a collection that *doesn't* include folk speech.

Because folk speech seems trivial and mundane to some, it can be tough to understand how it functions in society. My mentor Alan Dundes did great work here, collecting countless folk speech texts in the University of California Berkeley folklore archives. Once you've amassed thousands of texts, you can start to reasonably generalize about their meaning.

For example, Dundes asserts that American folk speech is very linear in nature. He writes that one of folklore's potential contributions to identifying the conceptual underpinnings of culture is that "native categories of perception are clearly delineated in various genres, including those subsumed under the rubric of folk speech" (93). By documenting the different connotations of straight/linear phrases vs. round/curvy ones, Dundes concludes that Americans do see the world through a linear lens, and furthermore that it's a gendered one, with logical/linear thinking attributed more to men than to women (and I have to give Dundes credit for this insight, since he never identified as a feminist).

We don't need to go all Sapir-Whorf hypothesis to acknowledge that language is culturally coded, and the language we use both reflects and shapes how we see the world. The study of folk speech can help us better understand our conceptual categories, and the underlying beliefs that influence how we move in the world.

References:

Brunvand, Jan Harold. *The Study of American Folklore: An Introduction*. Fourth edition. W. W. Norton & Company, 1998 [1968, 1978, 1986].

Dundes, Alan. "'As the Crow Flies': A Straightforward Study of Lineal Worldview in American Folk Speech." *"The Kushmaker" and Other Essays on Folk Speech and Folk Humor,* edited by Wolfgang Mieder, The University of Vermont, 2008 [2004]. 93-108.

PROVERB

YO DAWG, I heard you like proverbs, so I'm going to define a proverb with a proverb so we can proverb while we proverb. Or something.

The wisdom of many, the wit of one is an example of metafolklore (folklore about folklore). It distills the essence of proverbs into a proverb, emphasizing their transmission of communally-held knowledge in the pithy phrasing that probably came from a single speaker. In this post, I'll define and discuss proverbs, with bunches of examples, because proverbs are fun like that.

Like folk speech and jokes, proverbs belong to the overall category of verbal folklore, but they also cross genre boundaries. The next chapter, on Wellerisms, concretely demonstrates this. Proverbs also make their way into cartoons, comics, advertisements, and other forms of media. They can appear in other folklore genres, such as personal narratives or sermons.

We typically define proverbs as metaphorical statements of traditional wisdom. Proverbs are metaphorical in that they use poetic language to describe things symbolically. My favorite example of this is the proverb "Don't cry over spilt milk." We're not literally talking about milk here, but rather using it metaphorically to talk about regret.

Structurally, proverbs usually follow the form: topic + comment. In some cases this is incredibly simple, with one word representing each part of the structure:

- "Money talks"
- "Shit happens"
- "Time flies"

In many other cases, the topic + comment structure is more complex. In the case of "Boys will be boys" the topic or subject is equivalent to the commentary. In "Two wrongs don't make a right," the topic does NOT equal the comment but still follows it grammatically.

The phrasing of proverbs, normally studied as part of their texture, is often what we call fixed-phrase rather than free-phrase. Really short proverbs are less likely to exhibit variation at the level of word usage and structure, whereas longer ones might. But basically, once a proverb becomes traditional, it tends to retain its phrasing. It's always "Don't cry over spilt milk," not "Don't cry over spilt coffee" or "Don't cry over evaporated milk." But you might hear "You shouldn't cry over spilt milk."

Unlike other genres of folklore, many proverbs have authors that we can identify (here's looking at you, Benjamin Franklin). What makes them folkloric is that, despite their origin in literary or historical sources, they pass into oral tradition and begin to accrue variation.

You might be thinking "But wait, if variation is essential to folklore, where's the variation with proverbs if they're mostly fixed-phrase?!" I'm glad you asked! Variation is key to folklore but it occurs at more than just the textural level. Variation can also occur in context, in terms of when and how proverbs are employed. Variation also happens at the level of meaning. For instance, in the case of "A rolling stone gathers no moss" is moss a good thing or a bad thing? Does it represent the kinds of attachments that are desired, or the kind that hold you back?

We study proverbs in large part because they can give us insights into worldview. One of the aspects here I find most fascinating is proverbs that are current in the same culture but which contradict one another (I really want to call these pairs "dueling proverbs" but that probably isn't a technically correct or useful scholarly category). My favorite examples include:

- "Absence makes the heart grow fonder" vs. "Familiarity breeds contempt" (not total opposites but interestingly juxtaposed in my opinion)
- "Look before you leap" vs. "He who hesitates is lost"
- "Don't judge a book by its cover" vs. "You only get one chance at a first impression"

I'll conclude with another tidbit of knowledge: a proverb scholar is called a paremiologist. How cool is that?! One of my favorite paremiologists is Wolfgang Mieder. His work is pretty accessible if you want to look it up; I like his 2005 book *Proverbs Are the Best Policy*. I'm also a big fan of the proverb guessing game (kinda like Balderdash) called Wise & Otherwise. So, go have fun with proverbs!

References:

Brunvand, Jan Harold. *The Study of American Folklore: An Introduction*. Fourth edition. W. W. Norton & Company, 1998 [1968, 1978, 1986].

WELLERISM

A STITCH in time saves nine, said the mother of eight as she sewed up her husband's pajamas. Wait, what? Welcome to Wellerisms!

In the last chapter we defined proverbs as traditional statements of metaphorical wisdom. There are a few different types of proverbs, as well as proverbial phrases such as folk simile and folk metaphor (next chapter), dite (chapter after that), and so on. A major proverb-ish genre is the Wellerism, which I'll define and briefly discuss here.

According to Jan Brunvand, the Wellerism is "a saying in the form of a quotation followed by a phrase ascribing the quotation to someone who has done something humorous and appropriate" (97).

That's a bit unwieldy, but the structure basically comes down to:

- Quotation
- Ascription

- Action

In other words, a text would probably look like the following: *"Blah blah," said the XYZ as they were doing the ABC*. Here are some examples of Wellerisms (in Brunvand):

- "I see," said the blind man, as he picked up his hammer and saw. (probably one of the better-known ones)
- "Everyone to his own taste," as the old lady said when she kissed the cow.
- "Neat but not gaudy," said the Devil, as he painted his tail blue.
- "It won't be long now," said the monkey when he backed into the electric fan.

As Brunvand notes, common speakers include the Devil, a monkey, an old woman, or a blind man. So it looks like I've covered my bases in these examples! The origin of the genre name (though probably not the genre itself) is Charles Dickens's character Sam Weller in *Pickwick Papers*, who apparently used many of these types of turns of phrase.

The text with which I began this post – "A stitch in time saves nine," said the mother of eight as she sewed up her husband's pajamas – offers some clues as to interpretation and function. As with many kinds of verbal folklore, word play is a way to display cleverness, and thus earn social prestige. I'd argue that this particular item also reinforces the folk idea that women are the gatekeepers of sex: as in, men always desire sex (which is a shitty evolutionary psychology story if you ask me) and women must reinforce their boundaries against that ever-present desire. So, the canny woman is one who thinks up ways to circumvent her husband's sex drive and prevent burdensome duty-sex and the attendant possibility of conceiving yet another child to care for.

As I'm not a paremiologist (a.k.a proverb scholar), I'm not up on the trends in Wellerism research, so I couldn't tell you what other scholars have had to say about this particular text. But I do like how the text deals with sewing on the surface... and is structurally a stitched-together text as well. Sewing is explicitly in the content, while the form is also sewn together from a proverb with added verbal context. It's a nice parallel. Studying Wellerisms helps us see which units of expressive culture are thought of as discrete enough to be quoted or attributed, and which units of language they're paired with in order to make sense in a funny, ironic, or otherwise appropriate way. And that is a pretty cool thing when studying language, culture, and folklore.

References:

Brunvand, Jan Harold. *The Study of American Folklore: An Introduction*. Fourth edition. W. W. Norton & Company, 1998 [1968, 1978, 1986].

FOLK METAPHOR & FOLK SIMILE

Folk metaphor and folk simile are tough to define and distinguish, but that doesn't mean folklorists don't try! Here's a brief (okay, not so brief) intro to our classificatory schema.

Somewhere between folk speech and proverb lies a genre that is both imprecisely named and described "proverbial phrases." Here's what Jan Brunvand has in *The Study of American Folklore*: "Proverbial phrases...are never complete sentences, regularly vary in form as they are used, and seldom express any generalized wisdom; nearly all of them are metaphorical. Proverbial verb phrases vary in number and tense and permit the addition of adverbial modification" (94).

Brunvand goes on to call proverbial language involving "like" and "as" "proverbial comparisons." I find this terminology dissatisfyingly vague, and so I tend to go with a paired genre distinction that I learned in my folklore studies with Alan Dundes: folk metaphor and folk simile. While proverbial phrases and proverbial comparisons map to folk metaphor and folk simile, I prefer the latter terms because I don't want to throw around "proverbial" as an adjective when what's being described is not truly proverbial in nature (lacking the fullest sense of a proverb as a metaphorical statement of traditional wisdom).

So, here's how I like to teach this material:

Folk metaphor is a traditional saying with an implicit metaphorical comparison. Examples include:

- to paint the town red
- to get/have one's ducks in a row
- big shoes to fill
- biting off more than you can chew

Folk simile is a traditional saying with an explicit, exaggerated metaphorical comparison utilizing connective language to make that comparison. Examples include:

- as slick as snot
- as cold as a witch's tit (in a brass bra, in winter)
- clear as mud
- quick like a bunny

It's easy to document tradition and variation in most of these instances, especially since they're only fixed-phrase up until a point. For example, I can say "Man, those are some big shoes to fill" or "I'm worried about filling these big shoes" and still have a similar meaning understood, and still have those clearly be expressions of the same folk metaphor text.

Here's where things get interesting: traditionally, we've defined folk simile as a phrase that has to include the words "like" or "as" to make the specific proverbial comparison, well, a simile. But then we run into problems with classification when you get texts like the following:

- He's so greedy he would steal the pennies off a dead man's eyes
- He's so stupid, that he couldn't pour piss out of a boot (with instructions on the heel)
- He didn't have enough sense to pee in a boot
- You're so skinny, if you stood sideways and stuck out your tongue, you would be mistaken for a zipper.

No "like" or "as" means technically we might not be able to call these folk similes, so are we stuck with the yuckily vague category of "miscellaneous proverbial saying" or whatever?

As it turns out, no! My folklore colleague Kelly Revak has done great work on this topic, which I'm drawing on here. I had the good fortune of working alongside Revak in the UC Berkeley folklore archive, and recently she's been working as an archivist at the American Folklife Center at the Library of Congress (how cool is that?!).

Revak prefers "folk simile" to "proverbial comparison" as a genre term because it highlights both the traditional/folk connotations of the genre, and its connotations of comparison, exaggeration, and intensification. Instead of just using "like" or "as" to convey these things, folk simile employs the poetic devices of exaggeration and hyperbole through specific linguistic structures: connective words.

In terms of their structure, most folk similes look like this: subject, attribute, connective, vehicle. The sample breakdown would be He (subject) is as clumsy (attribute) as (connective) a bull in a china shop (vehicle), where the vehicle is the metaphorical illustration of the attribute. I hesitate to use "metaphorical" too much here since I want to maintain a clear distinction between folk simile and folk metaphor, but hopefully you get the idea: the vehicle is what illustrates the attribute by making it come alive in an image or sense that is not to be taken strictly literally.

Revak proposes that there are 9 main connective structures employed in folk similes. Here they are:

- *As…as* (as slick as snot)
- *Like* (he eats like a pig)
- *…er than* (slower than molasses in January)
- *More…than* (more fun than a barrel of monkeys)
- *(adjective) enough to (verb) a noun* (that's gross enough to gag a maggot)
- *Worth* (he isn't worth his salt)
- *Know…from* (he doesn't know his ass from a hole in the ground)
- *So…that* (he's so weak he couldn't fight his way out of a paper bag)
- *If…* (if brains were gunpowder, you wouldn't have enough to blow your nose)

Basically, our classification systems have to take into account variation (because duh, we're folklorists). Reifying the like/as definition of folk simile does a disservice to the inherent variations we find in the genre. Thus:

- He's so greedy that he would steal pennies off a dead man's eyes = He would steal the pennies off a dead man's eyes

- He's so stupid, that he couldn't pour piss out of a boot (with instructions on the heel) = He didn't have enough sense to pee in a boot

They're all folk similes, they just are venturing far enough into free-phrase territory that the like/as phrasing doesn't appear, and the "so…that" phrasing can also drop out as well. But utilizing Revak's underlying structure of connectives helps us see that as long as one connective remains to draw explicit attention to the exaggeration, it's still a folk simile. Additionally, this helps us maintain the distinction between folk simile and folk metaphor, since in folk simile it's the explicitly stated exaggeration that's significant.

In folk metaphor, comparison is more important, and it doesn't necessarily have to be exaggerated or explicitly stated, but rather can be inferred. So to take an example, we're looking at the difference between "being up shit creek without a paddle" and "they're so screwed they don't have the chance of a celluloid cat chased by an asbestos dog in Hell" (both courtesy of Brunvand, pp. 94-96).

I'll wrap this up because it's getting pretty lengthy, but again, folklorists are all about classifying expressive culture based on structure as well as content. In distinguishing folk metaphor from folk simile, we arrive at a clearer understanding of how language is used in traditional ways to communicate ideas, values, and meanings that vary between groups. These verbal arts genres enliven everyday speech, infusing shared understandings with creativity and connection.

References:

Brunvand, Jan Harold. *The Study of American Folklore: An Introduction*. Fourth edition. W. W. Norton & Company, 1998 [1968, 1978, 1986].

Revak, Kelly. "'As Easy as Collecting Feathers in a Hurricane': A Re-definition of the Genre of Folk Simile." *Proverbium* vol. 22, 2005, pp. 303-314.

DITE

WHAT DO we call metaphorical phrases that describe weather phenomena, like the devil is beating his wife? Read on to find out what this tiny folklore genre is!

When folklorists are classifying texts of folklore, what do we do with the following items?

- "The devil is beating his wife" (simultaneous sunshine and rain)
- "Potato wagons rolling across the sky" (meaning thunder)
- "Angels having a pillow fight" (when it snows)
- "God urinating" (for when it rains)

So, we know that traditional phrases might be sorted into the large, highly prevalent genre categories of folk speech, proverbs, and folk simile or folk metaphor. I think one could make a compelling argument that these kinds of phrases might be folk metaphor, because they contain an implicit comparison. But then, they seem to have explanatory power of some sort, whereas folk metaphors are purely descriptive?

Instead, we call this traditional genre the dite (pronounced like *deet* as in the first syllable of the word "detail"). According to Alan Dundes, the genre term was invented by Carl von Sydow, the same tireless folklorist who gave us the concept of active vs. passive bearers.

As Dundes points out, dites are functionally different from proverbs: "Unlike proverbs, which pass judgment or recommend a course of action, a dite simply describes or respond to one specific situation. Many dites refer to meteorological phenomena, for example, 'The devil is beating his wife' for the co-occurrence of rain and sunshine" (28).

Not all dites refer to the weather, though. Dundes reprints a note by Reinhold Köhler (1830-1892), who was a librarian who did extensive folklore research. Köhler's note, "An Angel Flew Through the Room," seeks to trace the older sources that might've fed into this expression.

One might say "an angel flew through the room" or "an angel has passed through" (note that this is free-phrase to a degree) when you're sitting in a room, and everyone falls silent at the same time. I'm pretty sure I've heard other dites to describe this phenomenon, but I'm blanking on them at present.

Köhler, writing in 1865, finds that the Grimms likely knew the phrase, and it was also known in Spanish literature. An essay on Finnish epic corroborates its existence too. What does it mean? Dundes suggests:

> The dite discussed by Köhler may be alluding to the "angel of death" who is thought to come to collect the

> souls of those about to die. Implicit in any case is the equation of death and silence. The "dead" are silent as opposed to the "living," who can speak. In this context, one would speak to ensure that all those present remain living. Presumably, the angel has passed through (the room) without stopping to seize an unwary soul. But whatever this bit of folk angelology may mean, anyone who researches it will have to begin with Köhler's original brief note on the subject. (29)

Dites may be a small genre of folklore, but they're still worth discussing. As expressive phrases to explain natural and social phenomena, they may offer insights into worldview as well as about the circulation of folklore over space and time.

References:

Dundes, Alan, editor. *International Folkloristics: Classic Contributions by the Founders of Folklore*. Rowman & Littlefield Publishers Inc., 1999.

JOKES

Everyone loves a good joke, right? Except for when you're the butt of it. Folklorists have been studying jokes as part of our academic study of expressive culture for decades now, and we've always claimed that jokes are serious business, for all that they can range from funny to cruel.

We consider jokes to be a distinct genre of folklore, often verbal (but not always – think of pranks), that exhibit the characteristics of folklore: they're transmitted in traditional, informal ways, and show variation along the way. But they're also, importantly, humorous, often intended to make people laugh. Who's laughing at whom, though, is an entirely separate question!

When it comes to the form, or structure, of jokes, a few types stand out. Some jokes are classified as folk narratives, that is, they tell a story, in prose. Among the major folk narrative genres, jokes fit best under folktales, which are fictional formulaic stories. As in, nobody *actually* believes that a priest and rabbi walked into a bar and had that same conversation in real life, or that a horse or duck walked into a bar to order a drink. Traveling salesman jokes are a great example of this type of joke, as are dialect jokes. The shaggy dog story is another type of narrative joke, with horribly long and ridiculous run-on plots, often ending in a terrible pun.

Other jokes are not told as stories, but rather in question-and-answer format. Jan Brunvand calls these "riddle jokes" and notes that they "come and go in fad cycles, usually centering on a single theme while they last" (123). Examples include the little moron jokes of the 1950s up through political and disaster cycle jokes, which I talk about in the next chapter. These jokes point at the timeliness of folklore: we didn't have light bulb jokes before the invention of electricity, obviously. And no one's telling Dan Quayle jokes anymore, because they're simply not relevant.

Still other jokes are visual or pictorial in nature, meaning we don't consider them a type of verbal folklore at all. One example would be the line drawing of a lightbulb that, when turned upside down, looks like someone bending over from behind. Accessories for pranks might also be considered a form of material culture (whoopie cushions, anyone?), while the act of playing a practical joke or prank on someone would be more in the customary realm of folklore (things people do, rather than things people say or make). April Fool's Day pranks are an especially interesting area of study, because they can tell us just how far is too far to go with humor.

I especially like to talk about jokes as exemplary of the characteristics of folklore – tradition and variation – because almost everyone knows jokes, and can easily picture these principles in action. As Lynne McNeill writes: "If I tell you a joke, and you turn around and tell it to someone else and the details change a bit, you didn't tell it wrong, you just told a different version of it" (8).

Further, studying jokes helps demonstrate the importance of context in folklore transmission and performance. McNeill points out how "that dirty joke's punchline might still be told, but in a whisper rather than a shout, depending on who's around when you finally get your friend to tell it" (24). Here, we see the distinction between natural and artificial contexts for folklore: in a natural (or unprompted) context, people are just doing their thing, telling jokes and stories or whatever, whereas in an artificial context, a folklorist or ethnographer has solicited the material. As you can imagine, these different contexts can impact how the folklore text is performed in that moment, just as there are many "natural" contexts that might also influence the delivery (telling dirty jokes at a family gathering in a whisper so an elderly relative doesn't hear vs. telling dirty jokes at a bar).

Jokes also illustrate social norms through their content, as many jokes are founded on stereotypes: about gender, race, ethnicity, nationality, occupation, religion, and more. Jokes are also a way of perpetuating stigma, and looking for patterns in which topics are acceptable to joke about can reveal societal stigmas. It's (apparently) okay to make fun of certain marginalized groups when you're in the dominant group; I'm thinking of jokes about people of color, immigrants, sex workers, and sexual assault survivors, who are all quite stigmatized by and vulnerable to the policies of the mainstream. Speaking out against these forms of humor often nets one the accusation of being humorless (bonus points for being called a humorless feminist).

While scholars are still debating why people tell jokes at all, the idea that they're an outlet for repressed anxieties or taboo concerns is still pretty popular (for an alternative view, see Elliott Oring's work on jokes; he has published multiple books and articles on this topic). Dating back to Freud, Alan Dundes explains this view as

---

> Where there is anxiety, there will be jokes to express that anxiety. A society with political repression will generate an abundance of political jokes. Indeed, the more repressive the regime, the more numerous the political jokes. In the United States, we have relatively few *orally* transmitted political jokes. Why? Because we have a relatively free press. It's easy to hear or read editorials lambasting political figures on a daily basis; we have little need for oral political jokes. (vii)

Indeed, I would suggest that one of the reasons for all the jokes around sex and sexuality in the U.S. right now is that it's one of the major hurdles we face in this country, in terms of the deeply-ingrained sexism, heterosexism, and transphobia that exist culturally and pervasively. The intersection of folklore and sex, which was one of the topics Dundes inspired me to study, is hopefully one of the major contributions I'll make to scholarship and society more generally.

Finally, I'd like to point out that jokes which are actually metafolklore – folklore about folklore – can yield valuable information about stories and ideas that have become traditional over time. Dundes relays the following example of a metafolkloristic joke:

> *It was a dark and stormy night and this guy goes up to this old farm house. He's a salesman and he says to the farmer, "I'm a salesman, my car broke down, and I need a place to stay." And the farmer says, "That's all right, but there's just one thing, we have no extra rooms to spare so you'll have to sleep with my son." And the salesman says, "Oh my God, I must be in the wrong joke."* (in Bronner, 82).

Dundes interprets this joke in the following way:

> One might find, for example, that the substitution of homosexuality for heterosexuality is particularly significant in the light of our culture's taboo against homosexual activities. The mere suggestion of such activities to a traveling salesman, the epitome of unrestrained heterosexual impulse, is so shocking as to call a halt to the story. In other words, at the very mention of homosexuality, the American male wants out because this activity is 'wrong': the salesman is in the *wrong* joke. (in Bronner, 82-83)

Thus, examining metafolkloristic jokes can tell us which beliefs have solidified into stories enough to be parodied, which points us in the direction of embedded commentary about appropriateness and social norms.

Jokes are a treasure trove of data about cultural values, power, marginalized identities, and more. To that end I believe we should all bring a hefty dose of awareness to our encounters with the humorous, and see what's left when the laughing stops.

References:

Bronner, Simon, editor. *The Meaning of Folklore: The Analytical Essays of Alan Dundes*. Utah State University Press, 2007.

Brunvand, Jan Harold. *The Study of American Folklore: An Introduction*. Fourth edition. W. W. Norton & Company, 1998 [1968, 1978, 1986].

Dundes, Alan. *Cracking Jokes: Studies of Sick Humor Cycles and Stereotypes*. Ten Speed Press, 1987.

McNeill, Lynne S. *Folklore Rules: A Fun, Quick, and Useful Introduction to the Field of Academic Folklore Studies*. Utah State University Press, 2013.

JOKE CYCLE

WHAT'S BETTER than one joke? A whole cycle of them! Here I define a joke cycle in terms of folklore studies, focusing on the relevance factor.

In the previous chapter, where I define jokes, I focus primarily on their formal features: the humor of jokes being expressed in narrative, or question-and-answer form, or visually, and so on. Here, I'd like to talk about thematic clusters of jokes that folklorists call cycles.

A cycle is a grouping of jokes that form around a specific current event. Typical events that inspire cycles include politics (Dan Quayle or Bill Clinton jokes come to mind), disasters (the Challenger explosion), and massive cultural upheavals such as immigration (as with Polish jokes). Cycles stay in circulation as long as the issue they address remains of interest to people, on either a conscious or unconscious level. The jokes in a cycle tend to exhibit interlinked themes that often come down to expressing a particular social concern.

As one example of a joke cycle, check out my essay on

World War II humor.[1] And, as a reminder that not all jokes are delivered orally, keep in mind that I studied the Obama/Biden meme cycle and co-authored a book chapter on it (Jorgensen and Lee). That cycle was very active at the end of 2016 and the beginning of 2017, and then mostly died down with a few new texts being generated by little sparks of relevance (e.g., it was all too easy to posit that Biden, even out of the White House, was still mocking Trump in various ways, such as leaving a sabotaged "Word of the Day" calendar with the word "covfefe" on it).

My folklore mentor Alan Dundes was, as a Freudian, drawn to the idea that "no piece of folklore continues to be transmitted *unless* it means something" (vii). He went so far as to state that this is true even if the speaker or audience can't articulate the joke's meaning, and perhaps this is because jokes serve as "socially sanctioned outlets for expressing taboo ideas and subjects" (vii). Folklore as outlet is one of the functions of folklore that we're so fond of discussing, and joke cycles play perfectly into this as they stay in circulation as long as they're relevant.

But relevance – or its lack – can kill a cycle. As Dundes notes: "The American penchant for novelty tends to prohibit any cycle from lasting too long. Any given cycle seems to gradually or abruptly be replaced by another. For example, no one tells 1940s 'Little Moron Jokes' in the 1980s" (vi).

Further, the serial nature of joke cycles is significant. Telling one elicits another. The performance of jokes in a cycle is often a display of verbal and/or cultural competence, a way of showing that the performer's on top of current events and has the best/funniest material at hand.

Folklorist Monica Foote treats Livejournal userpics as a type of cycle, based on inside jokes generated from within the community. This leads to insights about the origins of cycles being available in many realms of culture, even as the expression of the cycle is usually folkloric in nature. Foote observes:

> In addition to the sort of inside joke that we've just seen, cycles are also frequently drawn from popular culture. The line between folklore and popular culture is certainly not as clear as it might be, but for my purposes, popular culture consists of items introduced to a folk group from without (via television, music, books, etc.) whereas folklore arises organically from within the group that uses it. (31)

So, while cycles can blur the line between folklore and pop culture, especially once you throw in the concept of internet folklore, they're still of interest to folklorists. It's as though by paying attention to cycles, we have our scholarly fingers on the pulse of the people. Sometimes the people we study use humor to cope with tragedy, or respond irreverently to grim circumstances. But this is all part of the human experience, and hence worth knowing.

References:

Dundes, Alan. *Cracking Jokes: Studies of Sick Humor Cycles and Stereotypes*. Ten Speed Press, 1987.

Foote, Monica. "Userpicks: Cyber Folk Art in the Early 21st Century." *Folklore Forum* vol. 37, no. 1, 2007, 27-38.

Jorgensen, Jeana, and Linda J. Lee. "Trickster Remakes This White House: Booby Traps and Bawdy / Body Humor in Post-Election Prankster Biden Memes." *Folklore and Social Media,* edited by Andrew Peck and Trevor Blank, Utah State University Press, 2020, 129-144.

FOLK NARRATIVE

"FOLK NARRATIVE" is a term I throw around a fair bit, so even though it's not technically a genre – it's somewhere between a large category of folk and a genre – I thought I'd go ahead and define it.

To accomplish this, we need to break the term down into its two components: "folk" and "narrative." I'll start with narrative.

A narrative is a story, or a framed retelling of events in which something happens or changes. Basically, there needs to be a plot. A narrative is not a snippet or a list or a brief summary, though narratives (of course) can be summarized.

Now onto the folk part: if folklore is informally transmitted, traditional culture, then adding "folk" as a prefix to something means it partakes in this type of cultural transmission. It means you can prove that it oscillates between tradition and variation. We do this by documenting that a text or type of performance has multiple existence and variation (e.g., you can collect it from different narrators/performers/believers, and it won't be exactly the same each time).

So to show that something is a folk narrative, you need to demonstrate both its folk-ness (that it comes from folklore and not print culture, the mass media, etc.) and its narrative-ness (that it's a story, and not some other form of verbal folklore that doesn't contain any narrative aspects).

Folklorist William Bascom describes folk narrative as *prose narrative*, as seen in the three key genres of myth, legend, and folktale, saying that they "are related to each other in that they are narratives in prose, and this fact distinguishes them from proverbs, riddles, ballads, poems, tongue-twisters, and other forms of verbal art on the basis of strictly formal characteristics" (7). In other words, other verbal genres of folklore like riddles, proverbs, and tongue-twisters wouldn't count as folk narrative because they're not telling a story, though they are expressed linguistically (as opposed to non-verbal genres of folklore such as rite of passage, which are expressed in actions rather than words, though they may have verbal components to them). Oh, and I might consider ballads to be a form of folk narrative, because even though they're put to music, they usually do have a plot...but that's a discussion for another time.

Bascom also classically defines the big three genres of folk narrative, which I'll relay here (and each gets its own chapter following this one):

- *Folktales are prose narratives which are regarded as fiction* (8)
- *Myths are prose narratives which, in the society in which they are told, are considered to be truthful accounts of what happened in the remote past* (9)

- *Legends are prose narratives which, like myths, are regarded as true by the narrator and his audience, but they are set in a period considered less remote, when the world was much as it is today* (9)

Fairy tales get slotted under folktales, FYI, and you might be familiar with other genres of folk narrative too (like personal narrative and ballad, which also follow after the next few chapters). Epic is a bit of a wriggly genre, encompassing elements of all three major genres above, and it includes both well-known Western examples like Homer's work and *Beowulf* as well as a variety of East European and Asian examples that I've read about but don't know well enough to go into. Once again, these genre categories are often culturally specific; there might be folk narrative genres extremely well known in other cultures and time periods that are perceived as highly specific and set apart from other genres, and I just don't happen to know about them because I'm not omnipresent.

Finally, I'd like to point out that folk narrative and its main genres are analytical categories not native or ethnic categories. Amy Shuman and Galit Hasan-Rokem distinguish these as such: "Analytic categories refer to the scholars' genre classifications; the categorization systems used by particular groups are ethnic genres" (64). Genres are resources for communication, whether we're using them in a scholarly context and imposing our own language, or whether people are using them strategically to get a point across in their own contexts. Very few people walk up and say, "Now I shall regale you with a folk narrative!" So keep in mind that while the term's useful in a scholarly setting, it may not get much play elsewhere.

And that's the brief way to define folk narrative in folklore scholarship!

References:

Bascom, William. "The Forms of Folklore: Prose Narratives." *Sacred Narrative: Readings in the Theory of Myth*, edited by Alan Dundes, University of California Press, 1984, 5-29.

Shuman, Amy, and Galit Hasan-Rokem. "The Poetics of Folklore." *A Companion to Folklore*, edited by Regina F. Bendix and Galit Hasan-Rokem, Wiley-Blackwell, 2012. 55-74.

MYTH

MOVE OVER, Mythbusters. The folklore scholar's definition of myth is more inclusive, and of interest to atheists and religious believers alike.

Myth is a genre of folk narrative, or stories / narratives that are also folklore (being informally-transmitted rather than institutional facets of culture). In a nutshell, myths are sacred narratives about the creation of the world.

There's a long history of people associating myths with falsehoods. William Bascom, who has written pioneering scholarship distinguishing between the different genres of folk narrative, notes:

> An extreme expression of this view is to be seen in the proceedings of the Fourteenth Conference of the Rhodes-Livingstone Institute for Social Research, entitled *Myth in Modern Africa* (1960), where myth is equated with unverifiable belief. In the usage of folklorists for over a

> century, myths are not simply beliefs; they are prose narratives. (13)

Thus "myth" has had multiple meanings for decades now, if not longer, and it can be used derogatively, weaponizing people's beliefs against them. That's not the goal here.

It's important to note that myths are distinct from legends (see next chapter for more). Both are told as though true in the communities where they're believed, and both are narrated in the third person (as opposed to personal narratives, which are told in the first person). However, myths are set back at the creation of the world and the time shortly thereafter, whereas legends occur in time that we'd count as human history. Of course there might be some fuzzy territory, and different cultures define folklore genres differently; it'd be Eurocentric to assume that every culture's narratives follow our definitional patterns.

For both myths and legends, if the narrative accounts for the specific origins of something still in existence today (such as animals, geography, or customs), they're called explanatory or etiological narratives. One example of an etiological myth would be a Philippine myth about how the moon and stars came to be, after a spinster pounding rice placed her comb and beads in the sky for safekeeping while working, and the comb became the moon while the beads became the stars.[1] In contrast, an etiological legend might be about the origins of the will-o'-the-wisp, such as a Scottish text where a dead blacksmith could gain acceptance to neither heaven nor hell, but did get one ember with which to warm himself, and he wanders around with it to this day.[2]

My folklore mentor Alan Dundes would explain the relationship of myths and legend by drawing an hourglass on the board, and then drawing a horizontal line through its middle. The line represents the beginning of human history, and so the bottom half of the hourglass represents time that is prehistorical and mythical in nature, and the top half represents historical time, which would be recounted in legends. Folktales (which I will cover in a couple chapters) take place outside the hourglass, in the realm of fiction.

Here are some examples of myths:

- The Book of Genesis, from the creation of the earth through Adam and Eve
- The earth-diver creation myth found in various Native American tribes, such as the Blackfoot
- The Norse creation myth as related in *The Prose Edda*

There's a long history of myth scholarship, which I highly recommend to those who are interested in how religions work and where they overlap with folklore and narrative. From the sources below, *Sacred Narrative* is a great starting point.

As Dundes sums up the trends in myth scholarship, we can see an increasing interest in understanding myths in their cultural contexts:

> While nineteenth-century thinkers were content to muse about myths from the safety and comfort of their library armchairs, twentieth-century scholars often made a point of going into the field to experience firsthand the recitations of myth and their impact on living peoples. The substantial increase in the number of myths

> recorded from all over the world sparked new interest in studying the nature of myth. (3)

We've seen progress from the types of theories proposing that mythical beings are based on real people (called euhemerism after the ancient philosopher Euhemerus who first proposed the idea) to theories attempting to account for the relationship between myth and ritual, or between solar myths and the minds of "primitive" people. There are psychoanalytic and structuralist and feminist interpretations of myth. At their core, many of their methods grapple with the question of how much to interpret myth literally or directly, and how much to interpret it symbolically. But however you slice it, myth is, at its crux, a charter for society, as famously stated by pioneering anthropologist Bronislaw Malinowski (in Dundes, 193-206). As long as humans are telling stories about our origins, we'll also come up with ways to interpret them.

One of the major functions of myth is to validate social norms, to explain why the world is the way it is, to rationalize the social relationships and power dynamics of a given society. This is why it's essential to connect myths to their tellers, to not take them out of context and treat them like literary texts and nothing else (though obviously studying myths in order to better grasp literary allusions is a worthwhile pursuit). On some level, myth reflects culture, and while there's no universally valid way to explain what precisely that relationship is, keeping it in mind can help guide us as we attempt to understand myth's many meanings.

References:

Bascom, William. "The Forms of Folklore: Prose Narratives." *Sacred Narrative: Readings in the Theory of Myth,* edited by Alan Dundes. University of California Press, 1984, 5-29.

Brunvand, Jan Harold. *The Study of American Folklore: An Introduction.* Fourth edition. W. W. Norton & Company, 1998 [1968, 1978, 1986].

Dundes, Alan, editor. *Sacred Narrative: Readings in the Theory of Myth.* University of California Press, 1984.

LEGEND

IF YOU'RE the person in your friend group who's always debunking things on Snopes, you deal with legends even if you don't think of them in those terms!

Broadly speaking, legends are a folklore genre belonging to the larger category of folk narrative, or stories/narratives that are also folklore (being informally-transmitted rather than institutional facets of culture). While it's also common to see legends being transmitted in other media, such as the newspaper or radio or internet, legends are still considered folklore because they exist in multiple forms and variations that we can document, rather than as static texts that never change.

At their heart, legends are folk narratives told as though true. This is one reason folklorists also refer to them as belief tales. This applies to everything from the story of the hook to the Kentucky-fried rat to local cemetery hauntings.

William Bascom defines legends as "*prose narratives… regarded as true by the narrator and his audience*" (9, italics in original). He explains:

> Legends are more often secular than sacred, and their principal characters are human. They tell of migrations, wars and victories, deeds of past heroes, chiefs, and kings, and succession in ruling dynasties. In this they are often the counterpart in verbal tradition of written history, but they also include local tales of buried treasure, ghosts, fairies, and saints. (9-10)

Legends are distinct from personal narratives for a number of reasons, though both are ostensibly about things that actually happened. Legends are usually told in third person, while personal narratives are by definition told in first person; legends are more widely transmitted on a cultural scale, while personal narratives tend to have smaller circulations.

Similarly, while legends may overlap with myths (defined in the previous chapter), legends take place in historical time, while myths take place in the time of creation of the world. Myths are more likely to be attached to religion than legends, but even this distinction is a bit finicky, as we believe the etymology of the word "legend" comes from the Latin *legere* or "to read," meaning to narrate the lives of the saints. But as Alan Dundes explains, "there could be legends of Adam and Eve that would take place *after* their creation (which would be a myth)" (6).

One example of a legend involving mythical characters is the origin of the fairies or hidden folk. Folklorist D. L. Ashliman has collected a handful of legend texts on his website,[1] and one of the Icelandic versions has Eve ashamed of her unwashed, dirty children. She hides them from God's eyes, and he says that they will remain hidden, as the hidden folk. It is thus entirely possible that legends can deal with religious topics and characters, and so we're looking at factors like context and documented narrative patterns to help us distinguish legend from myth in some cases.

Since legends can be secular or sacred, we sometimes distinguish between supernatural legends (things like ghost stories and hauntings) and historical legends (ones that do not usually contain supernatural elements, but rather are based on real, documented events). Of course, these categories get confused when you wind up investigating things like Civil War ghost legends. Legends also tend to be migratory, as Jan Brunvand observes in *The Study of American Folklore*: they are "widely known in different places...but when texts become rooted and adapted to a particular place, they are said to be localized" (197). And because folklorists are giant nerds, we have created a migratory legend index to classify these narratives as they travel.

Many people today have heard of urban legends, which are legends set in a modern time and place, usually not with supernatural elements. Folklorists tend to refer to them as contemporary legends, since it's not just in current times that we have legends specifically tied to our circumstances, reflecting back our social anxieties and fears at us. Well-known urban legends include the ones about gross things happening in fast food, strangers in the home (like the babysitter on acid), and alligators in the sewer.

I mentioned Snopes at the top of this post, but I should state that folklorists don't generally concern ourselves with whether a legend has roots in true happenings or not. We don't care whether a legend is true or not; we care why it's compelling enough for people to tell and retell it. What about the plot speaks to the members of a group? Why now and not five years ago? Will it continue to be told in the future? And so on.

The study of legends is a time-honored one in my field, and it's also one with important contributions to make to the rest of society. We still tell legends, sometimes centuries-old legends, even with modern narratives competing for our attention. Most legends are grounded in the teller's reality, with a meaningful message (often a warning), and a plot hook that's hard to ignore. Studying legends helps us hone in on what frightens people – and in these turbulent political times, we need all the help understanding one another that we can get.

For those wanting to learn more, Jan Brunvand is a well-respected folklore researcher and authority on urban legends. I often teach material from his books in my college classes, because his work is both accessible and very, very intelligently done.

References:

Bascom, William. "The Forms of Folklore: Prose Narratives." *Sacred Narrative: Readings in the Theory of Myth*, edited by Alan Dundes. University of California Press, 1984, 5-29.

Brunvand, Jan Harold. *The Study of American Folklore: An Introduction*. Fourth edition. W. W. Norton & Company, 1998 [1968, 1978, 1986].

Dundes, Alan, editor. *Sacred Narrative: Readings in the Theory of Myth*. University of California Press, 1984.

FOLKTALE

From Aesop's fables to narrative jokes to Little Red Riding Hood, folktale is a folklore genre that academic folklorists define a little more precisely than many people expect...but we have our reasons. Such as two-plus centuries of folktale scholarship, and a few millennia worth of written and oral texts.

Along with myth and legend, folktale is one of the major genres of folk narrative that folklorists collect, archive, and analyze. William Bascom defines folktales as such:

> *Folktales are prose narratives which are regarded as fiction.* They are not considered as dogma or history...although it is often said that they are told only for amusement, they have other important functions, as the class of moral folktales should have suggested. Folktales may be set in any time and any place, and in this sense they are almost timeless and placeless. (8, italics in original)

This is pretty close to the definition I use when teaching folklore classes: that folktales are fictional, formulaic narratives. I include "formulaic" because they tend to include traditional expressions and repetitions, such as how things come in threes in fairy tales. They are often secular, in contrast to myth which is related to religious belief, and they are not often believed to be true, in contrast to both myth and legend.

Since folktale is considered a large umbrella-ish genre of narrative folklore, it makes sense to talk about the sub-genres of folktale, which are usually widespread enough to be worth talking about as their own genres. These include (among others):

- Fairy Tales
- Animal tales (tales like Aesop's fables with talking animal protagonists)
- Narrative jokes/anecdotes (as opposed to Q&A style jokes like knock-knock jokes)
- Fabliaux (comic and/or bawdy tales, usually from medieval French literature)
- Formula tales (such as the Gingerbread Man, aka the Runaway Pancake[1])

Fairy tales get their own chapter, but briefly here: they're folktales (hence fictional and formulaic, which in fairy tales usually means things come in threes), with the addition of magical elements, quests, and transformations, usually to the tune of the protagonist changing from youthful to mature, low-status/poor to high-status/rich, and from single to married. But there are always exceptions; tales like "Little Red

Riding Hood" are undeniably part of the fairy-tale tradition, though it doesn't end in marriage, and it doesn't even always have a happy ending. To see this in action, read a bunch of early versions of "Little Red Riding Hood," only some of which end with her devoured by the wolf. Again, when we're talking about folklore, we're inevitably talking about variation, so documenting multiple versions of a tale and then demonstrating where tradition and variation appear is one way to study the folktale.

Some of the folktale subtypes are less well known today. Jokes and anecdotes that were known in European oral tradition as jests about married couples and priests are no longer in fad. But as Jan Brunvand points out, numskull jokes, which "attribute absurd ignorance to people" (238), are still prevalent, often in the guise of jokes about immigrants or other stereotyped ethnic groups.

Okay, on to some folkloristic tools for studying folktales! I've written about tale types in relation to a Twitter trend (maybe we can resurrect it! eh? eh?), and here's my brief definition (though if you want more, go to the chapter on tale types):[2]

> The tale type system, pioneered by Finn Antti Aarne in the early 1900s and revised by American Stith Thompson in the mid-20th century and updated by German Hans-Jorg Uther in 2004, assigns numbers to tale plots. So "Cinderella" is Aarne-Thompson-Uther (ATU) 510A, "Little Red Riding Hood" is ATU 333, and so on.

In other words, yes, folklorists are *such* giant nerds that we invented a system to classify folktale plots by number, and we're still using it. Heck, it's useful – "Cinderella" isn't called such in every culture where it's told, and thus having a system to categorize folktale plots based on something other than the tale's title is essential for international research.

Tale types are useful for a number of reasons, among which because they help us track the transmission and performance of tales regardless of whether they appear in oral or literary contexts. This is a vexed relationship, which many scholars have debated. I tend to follow the assertions of fairy-tale scholar Jack Zipes, who writes:

> Fairy tales were first *told* by gifted tellers and were based on rituals intended to endow meaning to the daily lives of members of a tribe. As *oral folk tales,* they were intended to explain natural occurrences such as the change of the seasons and shifts in the weather or to celebrate the rites of harvesting, hunting, marriage, and conquest. The emphasis on most folk tales was on communal harmony. [...] With the rise of literacy and the invention of the printing press in the fifteenth century, the oral tradition of storytelling underwent an immense revolution. The oral tales were taken over by a different social class, and the form, themes, production, and reception of the tales were transformed. (10-11, italics in original)

The main convention in folktale scholarship these days very much follows Zipes's work, distinguishing between the oral folktale (also called the oral wonder tale) and the literary or written fairy tale. Many times the plots, motifs, and themes of the texts are continuous, while changing the context is enough to make significant changes in how the tales function, and what their textures are like (hopefully you recognize all the terms in this paragraph; most of them have their own chapters if you need a refresher).

In regard to the importance of context, Cristina Bacchilega incisively observes: "A tale told by peasants in Medieval Europe simply does not express the same desires or values as the 'same' tale written by a Romantic German poet...narratives often symbolize different needs and aspirations for different social groups" (6).

Bacchilega also famously called folktales and fairy tales "ideologically variable desire machines" (7). These narratives alternately function in liberatory and normative ways, oscillating between sending emancipatory messages and conformist ones. And these messages are more often than not gendered; Bacchilega is one of many scholars bringing feminist theory and queer theory to the table, in order to better understand the folktale and fairy tale's "narrative construction of magic as 'natural,' with an emphasis on the gendered implications for women" (6).

Folktales are important to study because as folklore, they reflect culture. However, once you're in the realm of fiction, just *how* is culture being reflected? Obviously once we depart from reality – with, say, talking animals showing up in a folktale – we need to account for how we're not seeing the literal reflection of culture at that point. So are we seeing metaphor, or symbolism, or a reflection of some subconscious aspect of an individual's or society's worldview? It can be tough to say, and this is one reason why there are multiple theoretical approaches to interpreting folktales.

Of course, folktales are also elusive in part because they're so amorphous. When folktales were documented in writing (since, again in European contexts they often had lower-class connotations), they tended to appear alongside other forms of narrative. Take Greek mythology: "Cupid and Psyche" is the same plot as "Beauty and the Beast" (in the ATU 425 family, dealing with monstrous/supernatural bridegrooms), but it appears embedded in Apuleius's fictional work *The Metamorphosis*. Similarly, Odysseus's encounter with the Cyclops, whom he blinds and outwits by claiming to be nobody, appears in a narrative we'd categorize overall as an epic, but the plot of that snippet is found in international folktale traditions around Europe (it's tale type 1137, if you were curious).

A number of folktale plots also appear in ancient Indian writings like the Panchatantra (a collection of tales that dates from the 3rd century BC). As noted, folktale scholar Stith Thompson has stated in his monumental study *The Folktale*, a number of studies (including those done by the Grimm brothers) "posited India as the fountain from which the European tales had all flowed" (379). The comparative impulse remains strong in folktale studies today, though we tend to be less concerned about origins than about context and reception more generally.

Whether certain folktale plots derive from monogenesis or polygenesis, we may never know. But we can study their paths of transmission where we have the documentation to do so, and we can analyze how they're reinterpreted in new media texts such as film, novel, and comic book. Folktales continue to be relevant to people in various situations, and thus we'll continue to find a balance between studying their history and interpreting their updated and revised versions.

References:

Bacchilega, Cristina. *Postmodern Fairy Tales: Gender and Narrative Strategies*. University of Pennsylvania Press, 1997.

Bascom, William. "The Forms of Folklore: Prose Narratives." *Sacred Narrative: Readings in the Theory of Myth*, edited by Alan Dundes. University of California Press, 1984, 5-29.

Brunvand, Jan Harold. *The Study of American Folklore: An Introduction*. Fourth edition. W. W. Norton & Company, 1998 [1968, 1978, 1986].

Dundes, Alan, editor. *Sacred Narrative: Readings in the Theory of Myth*. University of California Press, 1984.

Thompson, Stith. *The Folktale*. University of California Press, 1977 [1946].

Zipes, Jack. *Fairy Tale as Myth/Myth as Fairy Tale*. The University Press of Kentucky, 1994.

FAIRY TALE

DEFINING the fairy tale is a difficult task, but luckily I've got some awesome helpers to aid me, in true fairy-tale style.

Let's be clear from the start: *fairy tale* (two words) is the noun, and *fairy-tale* (hyphenated) is the adjective form. That's the current accepted scholarly practice, anyway. There's a lot in this chapter, so at the end I've got a TL;DR (too long; didn't read) summary.

Of the major genres of folk narrative, fairy tale falls under the subheading of folktale (see previous chapter). Folktales are fictional, formulaic stories, with a variety of characters and structures. Fairy tales are distinct from other folktales (such as fables and narrative jokes) in terms of their characters (and other motifs) and structures but also their functions, contexts, and more.

So, let's start with why fairy tales are usually considered to be folktales (and not legends or myths, though there's the occasional crossover): fairy tales are clearly set in a fictional version of our world, which brushes up against the supernatural in ways that are normalized rather than awe-inspiring or terrifying. Nobody thinks that a story beginning with "Once upon a time" actually happened or is a part of our history. Rather, there are conventions that govern how fairy tales portray the world, and these align with non-mimetic fiction. (Want more in this vein? Read Max Lüthi's classic book *The European Folktale: Form and Nature*).

However, the relationship between folktale and fairy tale is a complicated one. We would probably state that all fairy tales are folktales, but not all folktales are fairy tales. This is both because we consider folktale to be the larger, umbrella genre under which fairy tales are categorized, but also because of the historical relationship between the two genres.

Jack Zipes – one of the most prolific fairy-tale scholars of the last few decades – has a lot to say here. I'm going to quote extensively from *Breaking the Magic Spell: Radical Theories of Folk and Fairy Tales*:

> Originally the folk tale was (and still is) an oral narrative form cultivated by non-literate and literate people to express the manner in which they perceived and perceive nature and their social order and their wish to satisfy their needs and wants. Historical, sociological, and anthropological studies have shown that the folk tale originated as far back as the Megalithic period and that both non-literate and literate people have been the carriers and transformers of the tales. (7)
>
> As a *literary text* which experimented with and expanded on the stock motifs, figures and plots of the folk tale, the fairy tale reflected a change in values and

ideological conflicts in the transitional period from feudalism to early capitalism. (10, italics in original)

The rise of the fairy tale in the Western world as the mass-mediated cultural form of the folk tale coincided with the decline of feudalism and the formation of the bourgeois public sphere. Therefore, it quickly lost its function of affirming absolutist ideology and experienced a curious development at the end of the eighteenth century and throughout the nineteenth century. On the one hand, the dominant, conservative bourgeois groups began to consider the folk and fairy tales amoral because they did not subscribe to the virtues of order, discipline, industry, modesty, cleanliness, etc. In particular, they were regarded as harmful for children since their imaginative components might give young ones "crazy ideas," i.e., suggest ways to rebel against authoritarian and patriarchal rule in the family. Moreover, the folk and fairy tales were secular if not pagan and were not condoned by the Christian Church that has its own magical narratives to propagate… On the other hand, within the bourgeoisie itself there were progressive writers, an avantgarde, who developed the fairy tale as a form of protest against the vulgar utilitarian ideas of the Enlightenment. (15)

Cristina Bacchilega expands on these points in *Postmodern Fairy Tales: Gender and Narrative Strategies*:

[T]he "classic" fairy tale is a *literary* appropriation of the older folk tale, an appropriation which nevertheless

> continues to exhibit and reproduce some *folkloric* features. As a "borderline" or transitional genre, it bears the traces of orality, folkloric tradition, and socio-cultural performance, even when it is edited as literature for children or it is marketed with little respect for its history and materiality. And conversely, even when it claims to be folklore, the fairy tale is shaped by literary traditions with different social uses and users. (3)

The evolution of the fairy tale from the folktale happened in a specific time and place: Western Europe, in the 16th-19th centuries. There were strands of fairy-tale-like things swirling around beforehand, and in other regions too. Prime examples include:

- From ancient Greece: "Cupid and Psyche" which is basically "Beauty and the Beast" (more on this in the excellent book *Fairytale in the Ancient World* by Graham Anderson)
- From 9th century China: a story, "Yeh hsien," that's clearly recognizable as "Cinderella"
- From the European Middle Ages: there are snippets of stories that resemble fairy tales in a religious context, which Jan Ziolkowski brilliantly discusses in *Fairy Tales from Before Fairy Tales: The Medieval Latin Past of Wonderful Lies*
- From the Arabic-speaking world, because hello, *The 1,001 Nights/The Arabian Nights*

But again: fairy tales crystallized as a coherent genre during the early modern period in Europe. Major players were

Italian, French, and German writers and, wow, I wish I could go into that history in this chapter but it's already too long. The website SurLaLune, which Heidi Anne Heiner maintains, has a lot of great fairy-tale texts and history, and their page on early fairy-tale history covers much of this ground.[1]

Okay, just kidding one brief detour into history: the reason we have the term *fairy tale* at all is the fault of the French, whose fad for *contes de fées* – literally tales of the fairies – in the late 17th and early 18th centuries did, in fact, feature tales with fairies in them (fairy godmothers, fairy villains, and so on). But not all fairy tales have (or need to have) fairies in them. As I discussed in the tale type chapter, this is a huge reason why scholars look at the underlying structural components of a narrative's plot in order to group similar tales together, since it doesn't matter if a magic fish or fairy godmother is helping Cinderella get to the ball so long as the action is performed.

The corollary to that last point (that not all fairy tales have fairies in them) is that not all stories with fairies should be classified as fairy tales. When told as potentially true, they're more likely to be legends.

Because fairy tales cover so much territory and so many time periods, they're fair game for a number of academic disciplinary approaches. As a folklorist of course I'm biased; I think we get first claim on studying fairy tales due to their roots in oral tradition. Fairy-tale studies has become its own interdisciplinary field, but we all bring distinctive theories and methods to the table depending on where we got our start and our academic training. For instance, Andrew Teverson takes a literary approach to defining fairy tales which is nonetheless inclusive in *Fairy Tale (The New Critical Idiom)*.

Teverson writes:

> As a generic form, the fairy tale is a many-tongued genre, a cultural palimpsest; because even as it speaks of the time in which it is told, it carries the memory of the other times in which it has circulated and flourished. It bears the print of the hand that holds it, but under that print it carries the marks of earlier hands. Thus as we read the stories of Perrault, we see in these stories the lineaments of older, Italian storytellers; as we enter German forests with the Brothers Grimm, we are able to glimpse the lines of human transit that tie nineteenth-century Germany to eleventh-century India; and as we read the polished literary adaptations of Victorian Englishmen, we hear, or think we hear, an echo of feudal roots. The fairy tale may, as a result, seem timeless, but it seems timeless not because it has not history, but because it has too many histories, because it is plural and many voiced. (5)

I really like Teverson's framing here, as he highlights the multiplicity of the fairy-tale form. Now for his actual definition:

> A fairy tale typically deals with the experiences of a youthful protagonist engaged on a journey, or in a series of tasks and trials, that has been necessitated by a change in his or her status: the death of a parent, or the loss of a magical object. This journey or series of tasks takes place in an imaginative environment, peopled by strange beings and wonderful creatures, some of which prove

> helpful, and some of which become hazardous threats. Almost invariably, the progress of the hero is hindered by the actions of a dangerous opponent, such as a witch, an ogre, a wolf, a tyrant king, or a malignant stepmother, but equally invariably (that is to say, almost but not quite) the hero or heroine overcomes his or her opponent, completes the journey or the set of tasks, and in so doing, secures for himself or herself a more comfortable life, and a more socially eminent position than seemed possible at the start of the story. Not all fairy tales fulfil [sic] exactly this pattern, and the phenomenal imaginative richness of this genre is such that even when this pattern is fulfilled, it takes such varied and inventive forms that it is sometimes difficult to ma a fairy tale onto this bald schema. (32-33)

The upsetting and restoration of balance in the protagonist's life is one reason why I state that fairy tales usually begin with the dissolution or disruption of the nuclear family, and end with either the establishment of a new one or the fixing of the old one. As Bengt Holbek writes in his monumental must-read book *Interpretation of fairy tales: Danish folklore in a[n] European perspective (FF communications)*, fairy tales track the development and entwining of two protagonists through a series of clustered plot points or moves. Three of these major changes are noted in my bulleted section below.

Further, fairy tales communicate about life changes using magical elements as a code. Holbek notes:

> *The symbolic elements of fairy tales convey emotional impressions of beings, phenomena, and events in the real world, organized in the form of fictional narrative sequences which allow the narrator to speak of the problems, hopes, and ideals of the community.* (435, italics in original)

Thus, despite their clear departures from reality in many ways, fairy tales always relate back to the cultural context in which they're being told (or written). And I think that's a good point for me to end on, since for all the flights of fancy we see in fairy tales, they make the most sense when interpreted in context.

Whew, okay, this was a lot of information. Here's the TL;DR version. When I teach fairy tales in a classroom setting, I emphasize the following points:

- Fairy tales are:
- Fictional narratives about magic, quests, and transformations
- Oral and literary; elite and mass/folk
- About changes in the main characters
- From youthful to mature
- From low-status to high-status
- From single to married

Fairy tales are NOT:

- Universal, timeless, or ageless
- Just for children
- Apolitical

- Anonymous (usually)

In other words, fairy tales comprise a complex genre with ever-shifting terrain, so precision with language (and when referring to translations and editions, also a complex topic) is super important. Fairy tales have their own history, and while the genre is quite flexible and expansive, it's not so general as to be a vague or meaningless term.

I only got to cite a few of the amazing scholars who make up our community in this post, so make sure to check out the works of Maria Tatar, Donald Haase, Lewis Seifert, Anne Duggan, Pauline Greenhill, Kay Turner, and (with some reservations if it's published after 2000, for reasons that involve shouting at a conference panel) Ruth Bottigheimer. Cool folks in my generation of scholars include Linda Lee, Veronica Schanoes, Christy Williams, Brittany Warman, and Sara Cleto, all of whom you can look up online (most of us are on Twitter and have websites or profiles on university sites to direct you to our work). There are more, too, but I've gone on too long already in this chapter, arg! (and this is part of why I'm not providing proper citations for every book referenced here; they'll be easy enough to find with title and author alone)

Finally, I've made bunches of blog posts about fairy tales and written scholarly texts as well; it's easy enough to find me on Google Scholar, for example. And as always, feel free to reach out online to say hi or ask for help finding more resources!

BALLAD

WE'VE all heard of love ballads, murder ballads, queer cross-dressing ballads...wait, what? Read on to learn about all the good stuff folklorists have been studying for centuries.

A ballad is a narrative folk song, or, a song that tells a story and is folkloric in its origin and/or transmission. In this chapter I'll describe how folklorists define and study ballads, from their content and typology to their emotional core and structure. I'll wrap up with a bit about murder ballads, since those seems to be popular.

Recall from my definition of narrative folklore in its own, earlier chapter that: "A narrative is a story, or a framed retelling of events in which something happens or changes. Basically, there needs to be a plot. A narrative is not a snippet or a brief summary, though narratives (of course) can be summarized."

Thus, ballads are sung narratives, or framed retellings of events. Their plots vary in level of complexity, though, as we'll see.

When folklorists talk about ballads, we often focus on their traditionality and their emotional core. The word "ballad" comes from the French "ballare" for "to dance," since we theorize that ballad singing and dancing were linked for centuries.

Did ballads actually originate from a "singing dancing throng" as has been speculated? Probably not, and that speculation is a bit classist and ethnocentric. But singing and dancing are linked in some ballad traditions, as in the Faroe Islands.

In the classroom, I sometimes joke that ballad is like the bastard lovechild of fairy tale and legend. As we'll see, the subjects of ballads overlap significantly with those of fairy tales – royal and noble characters, romance, fairies – while they're often focused on violence like legends are, often with similarly unhappy endings.

Ballads have an intense emotional core, even as their narrative structure is often simple and mono-episodic. As my colleague Jason Schroeder has taught me, ballads express the intense emotional experiences that occur through major life transitions and situations. Specifically, Schroeder wrote in his dissertation that "if fairy tales are the folk's collective daydreams, then ballads are often their nightmares." Ballads convey the dangers facing people in liminal and transformative spaces of maturation and family creation (wooing a lover; getting pregnant; fending off a rival, perceived or real). The social and symbolic risks of identity formation are thus conveyed in the depiction of an unstable situation and its resolution.

Bawdy folksongs are quite popular throughout history, and I mention them here even though they're not all technically ballads. My colleague Stephen Winick has a great piece on them at *Huffpost*.[1]

Gender and sexuality figure immensely in ballads, and thus they're ripe for feminist and queer analysis. For instance, the ballad "The Handsome Cabin Boy" (which you can find versions of on YouTube) features not only cross-dressing but also a love triangle and an unplanned pregnancy. And a number of the versions of the Appalachian ballad "Who Will Shoe Your Foot?" hint at gendered kinship obligations. You can listen to older versions of this text and others from the Ozarks at the Max Hunter Collection at the Missouri State University website.[2]

But take the contemporary rendition by the band Rising Appalachia which quite emphatically states "Sister will kiss my red ruby lips / I don't need no man". What are we to make of that? I know what my inner queer feminist scholar wants to think...

English-language scholars tend to recognize three main types of ballads:

- British broadside ballads
- English traditional ballads (a.k.a. Child ballads)
- Native American ballads (those homegrown in the U.S.)

The broadside ballads, circulated in England starting in the 17th century, tend to be sensationalistic and gory. They provide an excellent example of the interactions between print and oral cultures, as they were sold cheaply and were easily available, permeating oral tradition and pop culture. The stanza form tends to be quite varied, and they're often narrated in the first person (whereas Child ballads tend to be more third person). The UC Santa Barbara English Broadside Ballad Archive is quite extensive, and has been digitized.[3] Go have a look, and marvel at the gory bits!

When we talk about Child ballads, we mean those classified by American folklorist Francis James Child (1825-1896). Child was a professor at Harvard who identified 305 ballad types in his five-volume work *The English and Scottish Popular Ballads*. Because of Child's work, we refer to ballads in this corpus by number (similar to the concept of tale type for folktale and fairy tale texts).

Famous Child ballads include "Thomas the Rhymer" (Child 39), "Barbara Allen" (Child 84; Pete Seeger's has performed this one), and "The Daemon Lover" (Jean Ritchie has performed this one too).

If you're ever in one of my folklore classes, watch out! Sometimes I'll play a recording of a ballad text and then have students search through the Child index (or the listings that appear on Wikipedia if I'm feeling lazy) to try to classify it. The exercise is a bit sadistic but I usually only pick ballads that appear within the first hundred Child numbers, so it's not actually that bad. /smirk

The content of Child ballads tends to revolve around family drama, tragedy, bloody violence, and the supernatural (though it's been noted that as these ballads migrate to America, some of the supernatural elements have dropped out). Other scholars have focused on the primary two or three characters in ballads, either the hero-heroine-villain triangle or just the heroine-villain dyad (I've been told David Buchan and Flemming Andersen are the people to read here). The narrative tends to open *in media res*, with the action already beginning. And the narrative focus has been described as "leaping and lingering," meaning abrupt scene changes and shifts to the areas of the most tension or heightened emotions.

Their stylistic structure tends to be in quatrains with an alternating rhyme scheme (like x, a, x, a) and featuring iambic meter in a 4, 3, 4, 3 ratio (I think that'd be a mix of iambic tetrameter and trimeter?) An example is:

- "Well mét, well mét," said an óld true lóve,
- "Well mét, well mét," said hé,
- "I've júst retúrned from a fár foreign lánd,
- And it's áll for the lóve of thée."

The thing about Child ballads is they're not just found in English-speaking lands. And ballad scholars from other regions have done their own indexing work. I'm thinking here of Danish folklorist Svend Grundtvig, who was a very influential figure in folklore studies over a century ago (Child based his classification system on Grundtvig's).

So when we're researching ballads, we usually check to see if they have a Child number first, and then go from there. Knowing whether there are other versions to compare a text to is an indispensable first step.

And that leads us to the homegrown American ballads. These ballads often arise in response to events happening in communities that need a chance to collectively mourn, process, and remember. (We're getting to murder ballads soon, I promise!) Typical topics for homegrown American ballads include war and other tragedies/disasters, along with character types like famous lumberjacks or railroad men, criminals, sailors, cowboys, and pioneers.

As with other studies of texts that fall under the umbrella of folk music, we want to record the tune as well as the words. We want as much information about the context as we can get. We want to trace variations and understand the lives of the performers. When new ballads arise, as they inevitably do, we want to be on the ground to record the events that inspired them and track the evolution of tradition.

And this finally brings us to murder ballads. The podcast Criminal has an excellent series on them, first on Pearl Bryan[4] and then on The Portrait[5]. Pearl Bryan was murdered in 1896 after a back-alley abortion gone wrong. Her beheaded body was found in a field, and thus the grisly tale of her murder was turned into a song. This is rather typical of American murder ballads: event inspires song, which inspires numerous recreations in performance thereafter.

There are tons more murder ballads out there, and true to folklore, they display immense variation. Take, for instance, three versions of "Banks of the Ohio," performed by Ruby Vass, Otis Clay, and Johnny Cash. It's all clearly the same song, but with quite disparate moods, depending on the instrumentation and pacing and other elements. And when I played these three versions for my Berkeley students this semester, they noticed just how disparate the mood of each text was, so it's a fun exercise in how the music of a piece can contrast with the lyrics, and so on.

The "feel" of murder ballads is distinctive enough to be mimicked in non-folkloric contexts, too. Hanging is a common punishment in ballads, as seen in the ballad "Hangman" performed by Jean Ritchie. From there it's not a huge stretch to get to the song "The Hanging Tree" as performed in the *Hunger Games* movies.[6]

Overall? Ballads function to commemorate and mourn events that impact whole communities. They provide a commentary on justice and vengeance, and perhaps give a glimpse into folk ideas about what is right and what is excessive revenge. They allow coded conversations about sexual violence, and about gender norms. Sometimes these gender norms are upheld, while other times they're subverted.

There's a lot going on with ballads, and they're a time-honored topic for folklorists to study. I encourage you to explore them more, such as searching for Broadside Ballads Online[7] or CSU Fresno's Traditional Ballad Index.[8]

Again, I'm indebted to my colleague Linda Lee for sharing her resources on teaching ballads with me. I'm also grateful to my colleague Jason Schroeder, a ballad scholar extraordinaire who's taken lots of time to chat ballads with me so that I can understand them better. Any mistakes herein are my own damn fault.

References:

Brunvand, Jan Harold. *The Study of American Folklore*. 4th edition. W. W. Norton & Company, 1998.

Greenhill, Pauline. "'Neither a Man Nor a Maid': Sexualities and Gendered Meanings in Cross-Dressing Ballads." *The Journal of American Folklore* vol. 108, no. 428, 1995, pp. 156-177.

PERSONAL NARRATIVE

Of course it's a bit of a weird genre since I like it so much, but personal narrative is definitely one of my favorite folklore genres, in part because it's one that everyone can relate to as an active bearer!

Recall that in order for a story to count as a folk narrative, it has to combine the elements of narrative/story (it's got a plot rather than being an abbreviation or summary of a plot, or just a list of elements) and of folklore (it exhibits tradition and variation, and comes from informal culture rather than institutional culture). Most genres of folk narrative are culture-wide stories, such as fairy tales, myths, and legends, which can have a broad distribution over a geographical area or throughout a time span. But that's not always the case with folk narrative, as we'll see here.

So what is the personal narrative? It's a story that is:

- Told in the first person, about a real experience that person had

- Variable in form and length, fitting to the context in which it's told
- Alive only as long as its teller is, though it might also be picked up by those close to the teller (family members, intimate partners, and so on)

Why is it folklore?

- An individual's personal narratives become traditional in their repertoire over time, exhibiting variation (in texture/phrasing, context, and so on), thus satisfying the definition of folklore as expressive culture that shows both tradition and variation
- Though the content is unique to the individual, how we construct stories is culturally determined, and the motifs and themes available to a given teller are also influenced by culture
- A personal narrative often includes folkloric texture, such as the use of formulaic speech, slang, and insider/traditional knowledge

The personal narrative is also called the personal experience narrative, and thus might be abbreviated as either PN or PEN. My notes from my folklore coursework are full of scribbles about PNs and PENs, depending on whose class I was taking.

We all have personal narratives; as such, they're one of the most democratic forms of folklore. In contemporary America, people have generally heard of other folk narrative genres such as legends and fairy tales, but they may not have any available to tell in their repertoire. But I guarantee you that most folks have at least a handful of personal narratives that they can and do tell. Common topics include the first time someone did or tried something; life-changing events or accomplishments; travel; humorous or embarrassing incidents (especially from childhood); or how one met one's partner / spouse.

My main mentor in the study of personal narrative, Sandra Dolby, has a lot of useful insights about the genre. She writes:

> Personal narratives are best heard as they live – on the warm breath of the teller, in the resonant shell of the listener's ear. Then their purpose is clear: like any literary performance, they are there to move us, to excite us, to entertain and teach us. In the world outside of academe, the storyteller's responsibility is simply to be an adequate practitioner of the literary genre he chooses. It is the responsibility of the listener or reader to be moved, to respond. Sometimes the narrator takes some of that responsibility upon himself; he is moved by his own story and performance, and his own response leads his listener to a shared emotion. (x)

Personal narratives have many functions, linked broadly to entertainment, education, validating cultural norms, exerting social pressure, and providing wish fulfillment or release. More specifically, telling personal narratives about travel or extraordinary experiences can invoke wonder, while telling personal narratives about trauma or tragedy can be used to provoke empathy or pity.

For those keeping a close eye on religion, personal narrative plays a huge role in religious cultures. The sub-genre of conversion stories appears widely. Various kinds of testimony might count as personal narratives. Priests and preachers employ personal narratives in their speeches. Believers might have personal narratives about their relationship with their deity, their prayers being answered, their desires being thwarted (but it's all part of God's plan in some interpretations).

The neat thing about personal narratives is that because the content is so individual – even as it follows broader cultural themes – these stories include both the sacred and the secular. Pretty much everyone has personal narratives, though not everyone polishes them up nicely and is known as a great storyteller. But we all have some unique stories to tell, whether those reflect our experiences as believers or atheists. And as an atheist/agnostic folklorist, I'm convinced that we need to examine these stories using rigorous academic methods, and not necessarily take the "I'm a believer now!" narratives at face value.

I know that stories this widespread and quotidian can seem beneath notice, but I truly believe that it's important to study the facets of daily existence that tie us together. Personal narratives have the power to connect people, even if only momentarily, and that's worthy of our attention.

Finally, as someone with a foot in sex education, I love how closely the personal narrative tracks with issues of pleasure, vulnerability, and risk. Dolby writes:

> When a person tells a personal narrative, he or she invites someone to know him, to know her, intimately, personally. Such a person is very vulnerable; he may be

> repulsed or misunderstood. Like physically intimate encounters, such verbal encounters carry the risk of rejection along with the promise of pleasure. (x)

Whether it's verbal vulnerability or physical vulnerability, revealing aspects of ourselves to a chosen audience is one way that humans connect to one another.

So basically, personal narratives rock and are fascinating and everyone should be more aware of them. If you're down with some homework, you could ponder your own repertoire of personal narratives and pick one to analyze with a classmate or a friend!

References:

Dolby Stahl, Sandra. *Literary Folkloristics and the Personal Narrative*. Indiana University Press, 1989.

FOLK IDEAS

What do you call stuff that is obviously folkloric in nature, but not clearly classified as a given genre of folklore? Especially when it's deeply connected to worldview?

Luckily, Alan Dundes has an answer for us. And like much of Dundes's work, it ties in to deeply held beliefs that are useful in making sense of the world around us.

In the worldview chapter, I define worldview as how a group:

> perceives the world and their place in it…worldview encompasses factors like morality, causality, ethics, aesthetics, and more. Our worldview is what tells us what is good, right, and beautiful in the world; what makes the sun rise and set; what happens after we die; who deserves access to which resources; and perhaps even who deserves violence.

We study worldview as it manifests in various genres of folklore...but what happens when you've got folklore that crosses genres, or could fit in multiple genres depending on context, meaning, or intention? What then? (other than the anguished cries of thwarted archivists)

Dundes suggests that traditional notions that are expressed in folklore, but which are a poor fit for established genres, might be classified instead as folk ideas:

> By "folk ideas" I mean traditional notions that a group of people have about the nature of man, of the world, and of man's life in the world. Folk ideas would not constitute a genre of folklore but rather would be expressed in a great variety of different genres. Proverbs would almost certainly represent the expression of one or more folk ideas, but the same folk ideas might also appear in folktales, folksongs, and in fact almost every conventional genre of folklore, not to mention nonfolkloristic materials. (123)

There are a number of folk ideas common in (Anglo) American worldview, according to Dundes. He suggests that they include the Puritan idea about salvation requiring suffering (e.g., medicine needs to taste bad to be effective), and the idea of unlimited good (there always being enough to go around), and the prevalence of linear and visual thinking and metaphors. I mean, just think about how "straight" is slang (or folk speech) for "heterosexual"... in a linear-loving culture, what does that imply about non-heterosexual people, hm?

Dundes also distinguishes between folk ideas and stereotypes, which he terms folk fallacies. It's common to see these circulated-but-usually-false ideas called "myths," which of course bugs the crap out of folklorists (since we use "myth" to mean sacred narrative about creation). People can often articulate folk fallacies, as they're "part of the stated premises of a culture" (130). But in contrast, individuals aren't always aware of folk ideas, and may not be able to state them aloud. Thus: "Folk fallacies such as stereotypes would therefore be part of the conscious or self-conscious culture of a people whereas folk ideas would be part of the unconscious or unself-conscious culture of a people" (130).

Distinguishing between the parts of culture that are consciously held, transmitted, and articulated, and those that are not, is of course tricky stuff. However, it's a good task for scholars to set ourselves to, and one with potentially helpful effects as we help to understand cultural misunderstandings and conflicts.

So if you're in doubt about how to classify an item of folklore, and it seems to convey a traditionally-held axiomatic belief about the world or human nature, keep in mind that you might be dealing with a folk idea. Once we identify and articulate it, we can study it, and perhaps even challenge it. This might be my activist side talking, but that's one way we make progress, like when we fight racist, sexist, and heterosexist notions about human nature. It's a good way to make an impact.

References:

Dundes, Alan. "Folk Ideas as Units of Worldview." *Toward New Perspectives in Folklore*, edited by Américo Paredes and Richard Bauman. Trickster Press, 2000 [1972], 120-134.

SUPERSTITION & FOLK BELIEF

IS CALLING SOMEONE "SUPERSTITIOUS" an insult? If so, why? In this chapter we'll unpack what the folklore genre of superstition is, and why rebranding as folk belief sometimes helps.

The popular definition of superstition is as a naïve popular belief and any related behaviors, often thought to be illogical and irrational. Some common American examples include:

- A black cat crossing your path is bad luck
- Step on a crack, you'll break your mother's back
- It's bad luck to open an umbrella indoors
- If you spill salt, it's bad luck unless you throw it over your left shoulder

In contrast, we define folk belief as any traditionally held belief. It's usually a belief shared by members belonging to the same folk group, or a belief that can be demonstrated to have multiple existence and variation, coming from informal rather than institutional sources.

What superstition and folk belief have in common, and why we might use them interchangeably as folklore scholars, is: each is a belief, practice, or procedure based on conscious or unconscious assumptions; further, they share the form "cause/sign, result" where something either causes or indicates another thing.

This is one instance where defining a genre by how it's structured can be useful. As Alan Dundes has articulated, most folk beliefs and superstitions have the internal structure *If A, then B, unless C*. This is why we talk about superstitions as being primarily about *correlation* and/or *causation*: they're essentially symbolic folk systems for understanding how the world works around us. To take the third example from above, you have an "if A, then B, unless C" statement about spilling salt. Sometimes "unless C" gets left off, so we might talk about the "if A, then B, unless C" format as the fullest form of a folk belief, which is why it's important to collect as many versions as possible for comparative research.

In many cases, these items symbolically share an association with sympathetic magic. In other words, their symbolic logic works either due to positing that like attracts like, or that once in contact, things/beings will continue to exert an influence on one another.

We also categorize superstitions by their content, or the topic they relate to. Here it's relevant to mention Wayland D. Hand (1907-1986), a folklorist who created the classification system that is now widely used in the study of folk belief. We at the UC Berkeley Folklore Archive use his system to categorize superstitions that have been turned in since the 1960s.

The main categories of superstition that Hand identified are (in somewhat condensed form):

- Birth, infancy, childhood
- Folk medicine
- Domestic pursuits (incl. eating, food)
- Economic/social relationships & love/courtship
- Travel, communication
- Death; magic, witchcraft, ghosts
- Cosmic phenomena, weather
- Animals, hunting, farming

Distinguishing folk belief from folk religion (covered in a few more chapters) is tricky, in large part because religion is based on belief. My sense is that we tend to classify secular things as superstition or folk belief, whereas things involving deities tend to get filed under folk religion. But then you get interstitial figures like the Devil, who show up in both...so, uh, it's more like guidelines.

Some genres can look or feel like superstition or folk belief, but we still classify them differently. The line between folk belief and ritual can certainly blur, for instance (we tend to characterize ritual as the symbolic enactment of belief). And there's dite, which is its own little verbal genre. Superstition and folk belief can be fairly direct expressions of folk ideas, such as ideas about contamination (5 second rule, anyone?) or probability ("lightning never strikes twice," which can be interpreted either literally or metaphorically depending on what kind of situation you find yourself in).

A special case worth mentioning is "weather proverbs," which Dundes argues are actually weather superstitions. Recall that proverbs are traditional statements of metaphorical wisdom. Similarly, folk simile and folk metaphor use decorative language to draw connections, but aren't about causation or correlation the same way that we've shown folk belief to be.

One might try to make a case that a saying like "Red sky at night, sailor's delight" or "April showers bring May flowers" are weather proverbs, but as Dundes argues, one would be wrong. These phrases sound proverbial, but they're an "if A, then B" statement, so they're better categorized as superstitions.

Is this stuff kinda ambiguous and fuzzy? Yes, yes, it is. But so is culture, if you hadn't noticed.

Thus, at the end of the day, I don't necessarily care if my students use folk belief or superstition when referring to the genre of an item. I do worry that superstition might be off-putting to some people, and imply judgment, so that's one reason to steer clear of it. At the end of the day, we all have beliefs - and in fact, our beliefs may contradict one another and may not always be as based in scientific evidence as we like to think - so I think we should give ourselves and others as much grace as possible here.

References:

Brunvand, Jan Harold. *The Study of American Folklore: An Introduction*. Fourth edition. W. W. Norton & Company, 1998 [1968, 1978, 1986].

Dundes, Alan. "On Whether Weather Proverbs are Proverbs." *Proverbium: Yearbook of International Proverb Scholarship*, 1984, pp. 39-46.

RITUAL

"RITUAL" is another of those terms in folklore studies that has a wide array of meanings outside our discipline, so it's crucial to disambiguate these meanings. Otherwise, we end up with something that's a term as empty as myth (in its popular usage)!

Folklorists study the spectrum of traditional culture from sacred to secular, and we do this in part by tuning into rituals. And we can do this regardless of our own orientation to belief and non-belief.

We define ritual as a type of traditional repeated behavior with symbolic weight. However, as Hagar Salamon and Harvey E. Goldberg point out:

> Repetitiveness is relative, however, for some rituals may take place only once a year, or once every several years (inauguration of a head of state), or at much longer intervals (the coronation of a monarch). These examples

> point to another side of the standardization of behavior, namely the existence of norms that define rituals in a detailed and strict manner and establish public expectations of correct performance. (122)

In other words, rituals carry with them the understanding of how to do them correctly or incorrectly. Granted, one could be a passive bearer of a ritual, and thus have a sense of what it's about but not be able to properly execute it. And when we talk about rituals as "repeated" behaviors, we have to keep in mind that the intervals at which they're repeated can vary greatly.

The fact that rituals must have symbolic meaning helps distinguish them from other realms of human behavior in which repetition is key. I follow Salamon and Goldberg in defining symbol as "a sign, something that represents (or 're-presents') something else" (127). Every time I brush my teeth or put my car in gear, there's not necessarily a symbolic aspect; the act represents itself, without a deeper meaning. Those acts are purely functional. What you see is what you get (yes, we could argue about the symbolic value of tooth-brushing in a culture like the U.S. where displays of medical care do carry meaning, and where teeth are viewed as symbols of beauty and morality, but let's not).

In contrast, repeated acts like singing someone happy birthday or saying "bless you" when someone sneezes are imbued with meaning. These acts convey information about the individuals and cultures where they're common. They "do" something in the world other than what the act seems to be accomplishing on the surface (e.g., being polite).

How do rituals "do" things? One important component here is the concept of sympathetic magic. It's the principle by which rituals, through causation or correlation, are perceived to have an effect on the world or the people in the world. It isn't strictly rational, empirical, or scientific in nature, which has led to a lot of judgey scholarship in centuries past, making out non-Westerners to be primitive, ugh. But there's an inner logic to rituals that employ sympathetic magic, even if that logic doesn't mesh with science-y logic.

However, the truth of the matter is that ritual functions on symbolic and cultural levels. It doesn't have to be proven to work in order to be effective. Whether that makes it akin to the placebo effect, or just a quirk of culture, doesn't matter.

We study ritual because it's meaningful to the people participating in it. Whether we're talking about religious rituals like Passover or the call to prayer, or secular rituals like knocking on wood or taking a moment of silence for someone who's passed, rituals are moments of cultural significance. Rituals occur on a large scale, as when an entire nation observes them (think of the pomp and circumstance of funerals for nationally-beloved figures) but rituals are also present in tiny folk groups like families.

One thing I'll note before wrapping up is that we distinguish between ritual and rite of passage in folklore studies, which we'll get to in the next chapter.

Ritual is a category of human behavior that encompasses many actions on different scales (both spatial and temporal). Are there any rituals you observe, religious or secular, personal or on a societal scale?

References:

Salamon, Hagar and Harvey E. Goldberg. "Myth-Ritual-Symbol." *A Companion to Folklore,* edited by Regina F. Bendix and Galit Hasan-Rokem, Blackwell Publishing Ltd, 2012, 119-135.

RITE OF PASSAGE

Rites of passage: we've all been through them, but what exactly are they?

If you've been born, or baptized, or married, or if you've celebrated a significant birthday with festivities and/or debauchery – guess what, you've experienced a rite of passage! In this chapter, we'll define rites of passage, describe their significance in relation to folklore and religion, and talk about why they're significant.

Folklorist Arnold van Gennep (1873-1957) defines rites of passage as "all the ceremonial patterns which accompany a passage from one situation to another or from one cosmic or social world to another" (102). In other words, a rite of passage is a transitional time in life when you attain a new identity, whether social, religious, sexual, occupational, or other. The rite of passage is the collection of ceremonies and rituals that moves you from your old identity to your new identity.

One of van Gennep's main insights about rites of passage is that they all share the same structure. As Alan Dundes points out, this is hugely important, because before van Gennep's work, "folklorists tended to consider different rituals separately. Accordingly, one might compile a set of birth rituals, another might investigate marriage rituals, and a third might explore death rituals" (101).

Wait, are we using ritual and rite of passage interchangeably now? Not quite. In my folklore classes (and in the previous chapter), I describe rituals as the building blocks that make up rites of passage. Recall that rituals are traditional repeated behaviors with symbolic weight. If you think about a birth ritual being a traditional symbolic action that accompanies birth, then yeah, it makes sense to call it a ritual. But when you conceptualize the ceremonies and rituals around birth as *accomplishing something* in the social and/or spiritual lives of the people involved, you've arrived at the rite of passage.

Van Gennep was well aware of this problem, and took what we would now call a structuralist approach to disambiguating ritual (or as he calls it, rite) from rite of passage:

> Marriage ceremonies include fertility rites; birth ceremonies include protection and divination rites; funerals, defensive rites, initiations, propitiatory rites; ordinations, rites of attachment to the deity. All these rites, which have specific effective aims, occur in juxtaposition and combination with rites of passage–and are sometimes so intimately intertwined with them that it is impossible to distinguish whether a particular ritual is, for example, one of protection or of separation (103).

So, if even the experts are agreeing that ritual and rite of passage can be difficult to tell apart, well, there you have it. But that doesn't mean you should just toss the words around willy-nilly... that'll annoy folklorists and anthropologists everywhere. Make an honest effort to understand how the folkloric custom in question functions for its performers, and that'll lead you closer to an accurate answer.

Further, one of van Gennep's major contributions to this discussion is structural in nature. Rituals tend to be single acts, actions, or instances of behavior, while rites of passage are complex enough to have a tripartite structure. Van Gennep observed that rites of passage usually have three main parts:

- Separation
- Liminality
- Reincorporation

Since weddings are a classic example of a rite of passage, we'll use them to illustrate the three-part structure of rites of passage. In the separation phase, the engaged couple are taken out of their former social category – single people – and treated differently. In the contemporary American context, this would include things like the bridal shower, the deference with which the engaged couple are treated when tasting cakes and trying on outfits, and so on. We might even consider the separation phase beginning during the engagement, when a blingin' ring sets apart a formerly-single person as a now-taken person (and why yes, these rites of passage are often gendered, and can be ickily heteronormative). In other cultures, the duration of the betrothal period might be long or short, low-key or intense. Sometimes separation rites include things like ritual fasts or purifications, or different forms of dress a.k.a. body art.

In the liminal phase, it's a carnivalesque time of festivities, when the normal social rules don't apply (think bachelor/bachelorette parties). Liminality refers to a time on the threshold, betwixt and between. Usually, the immediate lead up to the wedding would be considered the liminal phase, when the engaged couple are shedding their identity as single folks, but they're not quite married yet. In early modern European cultures, there was often ribald jesting and riddling during the liminal phase of the pre-wedding festivities. Highly sexually suggestive jokes and folk dramas emphasized that this was not a normal moment in social time, but rather something special. If it looks like boundaries are being transgressed or the normal rules of social etiquette don't apply (but it's temporary so it's okay), then chances are good we're looking at a liminal phase. For instance, at many American wedding receptions the bride and groom smush wedding cake into each other's faces… which is not normal food etiquette, right? Nor do most people in their daily lives toss garters or bouquets or flowers at random strangers in a crowd.

The reincorporation phase involves folding the newly-married couple back into normal social life, and emphasizing their now-married status. Some of the rituals observed after the wedding ceremony – the couples dance, toasting to the newly married couple – are meant to solidify this status. Many weddings take place in a house of worship but then move to a secular space for the celebration, which would exemplify the shift from a liminal to reincorporation phase (things going from abnormal back to normal, though a new version of normal). Perhaps even returning to "normal" society after a honeymoon, or having changed one's name, could be considered parts of the reincorporation phase.

The advantage of the tripartite structure that van Gennep

identified is that it unifies all rites of passage, regardless of which part of life they govern, or which culture they come from. Most rites of passage follow this structure, and indeed, this structure can be useful in distinguishing rites of passages from rituals that happen to occur at a time of significant life change. Whether we're talking about birth as a rite of passage (welcome to this world), graduation, marriage, starting or ending a career, or a funeral (leaving this world), many rites of passage are similarly structured, and we can use this insight to better understand them as a whole.

Because all of us have been born, we've all experienced birth as a rite of passage. Many of us have experienced subsequent ones, such as graduating, celebrating reaching adolescence and/or adulthood (any special plans when you turn 16 or 18 or 21 in the U.S., hm?), and so on. Whether sacred or secular, rites of passage help us track the social and spiritual dimensions of our life cycle, and they bind us to each other and our communities. Structured in three main parts, rites of passage also incorporate significant elements of identity, and thus are worth discussion and study.

References:

Dundes, Alan, editor. *International Folkloristics: Classic Contributions by the Founders of Folklore*. Rowman & Littlefield Publishers Inc., 1999.

Van Gennep, Arnold. "The Rites of Passage." *International Folkloristics: Classic Contributions by the Founders of Folklore*, edited by Alan Dundes, Rowman & Littlefield Publishers Inc., 1999, 99-108.

OSTENSION

IF YOU'VE HEARD of the Slenderman murder attempt, you've heard of ostension.

At one point I was writing about legends, and a friend asked about that phenomenon where people enact legends they've heard or read about. I was like, oh, you mean ostension? Hence this post.

Folklorist Carl Lindahl defines ostension as "the process through which people live out legend, making it real in the most palpable sense" (164). This includes a range of motivations, from those "calculatingly conscious…or the result of an unconscious, delusional compulsion" (164). Building on the foundational work of Linda Dégh, who first began studying ostension in the early 1980s, a number of folklore scholars have brought nuance to this important concept, studying everything from pilgrimages to legend-imitating murders to Halloween candy scares.

Specific examples of ostension include:

- Going to visit a haunted cemetery or haunted house
- Making a pilgrimage to a site that is sacred to a saint or deity
- Trying/testing out legendary exploits like on the TV show *Mythbusters*
- Mutilating cattle or other animals, as happened in the 1970s in Ohio and was attributed to cults and/or UFOs (discussed in the Ellis reference)
- Visiting the haunted train tracks in San Antonio, as Lindahl explores in his article (which also features a "gravity hill," where you put your car in neutral and it's supposed to slowly roll uphill)
- The Slenderman murder attempt, of course

Andrew Peck (one of my folklore colleagues), in his study of the Slenderman legend, describes it as "a digital legend cycle that combines the generic conventions and emergent qualities of oral and visual performance with the collaborative potential of networked communication" (334). In other words, it's a prime example of digital folklore, one that emerged in 2009 on the SomethingAwful forums and has since appeared in multiple expressive modes (visual media, blog posts, Halloween costumes, pranks, and ostension).

The lines between legend and reality sometimes blur, which is why it's important to have the concept of ostension as part of the conversation. Folklorist Bill Ellis also uses the term pseudo-ostension (imitating a traditional narrative in order to create a hoax), in this instance in an article about murders as ostension. He notes that in the case of a particular crime: "One possibility is that the crime was a form of pseudo-ostension: that is, satanism had nothing to do with the murder itself but everything to do with how the murderer intended his crime to be seen by the community. Thus the crime came first, folklore second" (213).

Ellis's article contains some truly macabre examples of crimes – from kidnapping and killing infants to mutilating the corpses of animals and humans – so keep that in mind if you decide to track it down. He reminds us that "traditional narratives exist not simply as verbal texts to be collected, transcribed, and archived. They are also maps for action, often violent actions" (218). Discussing ostension is a good reminder that although we tend to consider legends in the context of folk narrative, or verbal folklore in story form, legends span into belief and action as well. In other words, legends don't stay put in tidy boxes. They resist easy classification.

As another example of genre collapse, we tend to say that legends are told in the third person and personal narratives are told in the first person, but both are generally regarded as true. But what about when someone hears a legend, decides to go enact it (thus putting ostension into play) and then they wind up with a personal narrative about the experience? How do we map that one out?

These questions have vital importance to everyday life. When the Slenderman murder attempt occurred, Peck was consulted by dozens of media personalities and outlets to bring some perspective to the issue. He wrote of the experience:

> I spent most of June explaining…that concerns over Slender Man were largely overblown – akin to scrutinizing children's mirror use for fear of Bloody Mary – and distracting from many more real dangers

> young people may face online. [...] Further study of the Slender Man in wake of these events could yield valuable insight into ostentive behaviors, media uptake of legend cycles, and the circulation of urban legends among young people in the digital age. As folklorists, we are keenly positioned to explore and weigh in on these issues (346-347).

Like Peck, I believe that studying ostension can help inform larger questions regarding culture in the age of the internet, and risk assessment when it comes to young people. I've noticed a pattern of rhetoric designed to get people worked up about issues that don't impact as many people as the issues that folks are loathe to discuss. For instance, where's the furor over how lack of access to comprehensive sex ed is leaving young people vulnerable to predation and unwanted pregnancies, or how intolerance is leading LGBTQ youth to be facing homelessness in high numbers? Far easier to get worked up over kids these days and their urban legends.

Ostension provides us with a handy term to conceptualize the translation from legend into action, regardless of degrees of veracity and intention. It is a scholarly agnostic term, designed to be descriptive, to facilitate analysis even when facets of the act remain mysterious. As digital media and legends continue to collide, keeping ostension in mind will help us get a handle on the complexities of belief, narrative, and action.

References:

Ellis, Bill. "Death by Folklore: Ostension, Contemporary Legend, and Murder." *Western Folklore* vol. 48, no. 3, 1989, pp. 201-220.

Lindahl, Carl. "Ostentive Healing: Pilgrimage to the San Antonio Ghost Tracks." *Journal of American Folklore* vol. 118, no. 468, 2005, pp. 164-185.

Peck, Andrew. "Tall, Dark, and Loathsome: The Emergence of a Legend Cycle in the Digital Age." *Journal of American Folklore* vol. 128, no. 509, 2015, pp. 333-348.

FOLK MUSIC & FOLK SONG

FOLK MUSIC and folk song are giant topics which I won't do justice to here, but as they occupy a huge realm of human experience, I'll certainly try!

My music training happened a long time ago, so I always get massive impostor syndrome feels when teaching about music as an academic subject, but here goes! In folklore studies we define folk music as:

- A culture's informally transmitted, traditional musical practices
- Perpetuated in oral tradition regardless of origins
- That encompasses instrumental music, music with words, whole genres, and social contexts

Okay, let's unpack this. What's key about folk music being *folk* is variation. As with many kinds of folklore, we don't necessarily care about origins, but rather how it's transmitted.

So while some folk music starts out with a definite author, as part of elite or "high art" culture, if it passes into oral tradition that produces variants, we consider it folk music. We're interested in communities recreating these texts in ways that are folkloric in nature.

As someone who did her folklore graduate work at Indiana University, where folklore and ethnomusicology share a department, I've been known to cheekily say that I'm still not sure whether ethnomusicology is the study of culture through music, or the study of music through culture. The point is a similar one for folklore studies: we're interested in the study of music through the lens of what counts as folklore, or perhaps in the study of folklore through music… I'm not quite sure which, or whether it matters. The American Folklife Center at the Library of Congress puts out regular publications on the topic, and has an excellent online guide to the history of folk music and folk song collection in the U.S., which goes into more detail about how all these things relate.[1]

It's also important to note that we differentiate folk music as a scholarly category denoting a genre of folklore from the stuff that record companies label as "folk music." There are some clear connections between the development of the American "folk music" scene and the study of folk music, but this is totally not my area of expertise, so I'm going to recommend that you explore the American Folklife Center's blog about folk music if you want to know more.[2]

Folk music is damn near universal, which makes it really interesting to discuss and study. Pretty much every culture has rhythmic patterns, instruments, and songs that are unique to it, or that are transmitted there from elsewhere that latch on and produce homegrown variants.

As an example of the importance of context to the study of folk music, we might talk about how certain situations give rise to folkloric musical practices that are tough to define, but still clearly folkloric in nature. As in, situations where people gather to play music or sing, even if that music isn't clearly folk music according to a strict genre breakdown. An instance might be studying a drum circle in America where there's no clearly defined genre other than something vague like "African drumming" or "Middle Eastern drumming" but we want to understand how the musicians come together and share knowledge and techniques.

Further, while it's difficult to distinguish between folk music and folk song, we tend to define folk song in the following way:

- Words and music that circulate orally in traditional variants among members of a folk group
- Regardless of their origins (as high/art music or pop music)
- Including wordless folk songs, or traditional melodies like "shave and a haircut (two bits)"

While ballads get their own chapter above in the more solidly verbal folklore genres section, here are some major types of folk songs:

- Narrative songs (usually called ballads)
- Functional songs, or songs paired with a purpose (lullabies, work songs, children's game songs)
- Lyrical folk songs (traditional songs that express a mood or feeling without having the plot of a

narrative song, like blues/spirituals, drinking songs, or protest songs)

Some folk songs are fixed-phrase, whereas others are free-phrase. In other words, the words of the text may be more or less static depending on which one we're talking about. Most of the parodies of "Jingle Bells," for example, need to start with those two words, making that opening formula, at least, fixed phrase (regardless of whether we go on to say that Batman smells). And since almost everyone in America recognizes the tune of the "Happy Birthday" song, that gives us leeway to change the words to parody, and still have it be recognizable. But deviate too far, and you might veer into creation of a new song.

Folk music and folk dance (see next chapter) are, of course, closely related in many cultures. The go-to example for me as a belly dancer is how many types of Middle Eastern dance evolved in connection with music of those regions; since Egyptian music sounds different than Turkish music, of course Egyptian dance looks different than Turkish dance. This is in part because of time signature, with much Egyptian music being in 4/4 and much Turkish music being in 9/8. You *have to* dance differently when that's the case!

Finally, we can't talk about folk music without talking about the collecting and scholarship of Alan Lomax. The American Folklife Center has a page devoted to the centennial celebration of his birthday, which has a ton of resources.[3]

Special thanks go to my colleague Linda Lee for sharing her lecture notes with me. We both base a lot of our teaching on this topic on the Brunvand book cited below.

References:

Brunvand, Jan Harold. *The Study of American Folklore: An Introduction*. Fourth edition. W. W. Norton & Company, 1998 [1968, 1978, 1986].

FOLK DANCE

Folk dance is a large and amorphous topic, but as with any field that studies the human body's relationship to culture, it offers vital and intriguing insights.

As both a dancer and a scholar of dance, I'm always thrilled to talk about dance. But what makes a dance a folk dance? I've got some criteria to list here.

First, we have to define dance, which is no small task. Dance anthropologist Anya Royce (with whom I took classes while doing my graduate work at Indiana University) defines dance as "the body making patterns in time and space."

This is a broad definition. I like it because it can refer to things we might not normally think of as dance, like yoga and tai chi and walking a labyrinth. However, I like to consider dance as having additional elements to it, something like intention or the interplay of creativity and constraint.

So if dance is patterned movement (likely with intentional and/or artistic elements), folk dance would be dance that also meets the criteria of folklore as expressive culture. Folklore is informally transmitted traditional culture, often sorted into genres by its practitioners (though scholars may have another take on categorizing genres). Folk dance, then, is patterned movement that we can observe unfolding within a folk group and being transmitted through less-institutional means, retaining relevance to the people who practice it.

Examples of folk dance might include the dances we learn from our families, from our peers, and in other informal situations. When explaining this concept to students, I might ask them how people dance at the weddings they attend, and where they learned these dances. If the answer about origins is fuzzy, it's probably a folk dance since it's just how "everyone" dances. Folk dance is not incompatible with technology, either; while technology preserves dances in a visual way that has only recently become accessible to humanity, you have only to look at TikTok dances to see tradition and variation at work. Certainly many forms of folk dance are now commercialized, such that we pay to take classes and attend organized events. But in order to be considered folk dance, these dance forms must retain a connection to tradition. They can't be all-commercial all-the-time, or such highly codified forms (like ballet) that only those who've paid to study since childhood have a shot at learning and performing these styles.

The informality central to folk dance doesn't mean that dancers of all styles don't have their own folklore. I'd argue that for all that ballet's not a folk dance (at least not currently), the folk group of ballet dancers probably has a lot of shared folklore (customs, dress, and so on). My favorite dance style to practice, teach, and perform, FatChance BellyDance style, is a contemporary American take on the folk dances of the Middle East and North Africa, and while it's become somewhat stylized and commercialized, it still offers many folk dance elements such as informally shared cultural practices.

While the performance of dance is unarguably appealing and compelling, there's more to talking about folk dance than talking about its performance. Performance studies can offer a valuable lens through which to observe the emergent nature of dance, but it's also useful to investigate the body art associated with dance (such as costumes and body-sculpting strategies), the personal narratives that dancers tell, the customs and etiquette of various dance communities, and so on.

Folk dance has different meanings in different contexts, though. The Society of Folk Dance Historians offers a multifaceted definition of folk dance, relying on the devolutionary premise to categorize dances as either "folkloric" or "folky" in nature (the former serve a metaphysical purpose in their communities; the latter have lost their original intent but are still traditionally performed).[1] I'm not too hung up on this distinction, given that I tend to view the transmission process, not the intent, as what makes something folkloric in nature.

One of the best reasons for studying folk dance is that it is a way to visually and kinesthetically display identity. Many early studies of folk dance focused on emerging nationalist movements and how folk dances represented nationalistic identities. Gender is another identity prominently displayed in dance. As I argued in my keynote on the body in folklore,[2] folk dance often is based on constructions of ethnicity and nationality...which means it's also problematic at times:

> [T]he bodily constructions in body art and folk dance are subject to stereotypes, stigma, and other forms of folk belief. These assessments impact how we view others,

> and how we ourselves are viewed, forming a part of a coherent cultural whole about which bodies are welcomed into which spaces, and which are treated with disdain if not outright violence.

The constraints laid upon gendered and sexualized dancing bodies – how it's appropriate or inappropriate or even legal to move, see, and be seen – are yet another reminder that dance is a pathway to cultural values. As a belly dancer, I'd be remiss in not mentioning how the local interpretations of Islamic law impact whether women can dance publicly in the Middle East and North Africa, and what their costume options are. In some folk dances, men and women have completely different movement vocabularies accessible to them. I'm thinking of Polynesian dance in particular; there are notable differences between Tahitian men's and women's dancing (and speaking of gendered movement vocabularies, I love to show my classes videos of Hawaiian men's dancing because most American students don't expect men to be able to move their hips like that…gender norms at work, y'all!).

Studying folk dance gives us a way to understand what people think is traditional and true about bodies (gendered, ethnic, and so on). Folk dance is often more egalitarian and accessible than other dance forms, especially elite ones like ballet, but it still constructs and represents bodies in particular ways, and as cultural scholars, that's what we're into analyzing. It doesn't hurt that studying dance is also engaging and fun!

FOLK RELIGION & VERNACULAR RELIGION

Folklore and religion intersect at multiple points, maybe more than you'd think. How various cultures conceptualize the connections between the human and the divine can help us understand what people value, fear, and love.

Folklorists are not necessarily interested in the whole of religion, but rather the parts of it that meet the definition of folklore: informal, traditional culture. We call this folk religion, religious folklife, or vernacular religion. We study everything from religious texts that exhibit folkloric variation to folk groups organized around religious belief and practice.

But what is religion to begin with? All scholars of religion, whatever their home discipline, run into this problem. Typical approaches from past centuries distinguish religion from both magic (seen as primitive, irrational) and science (modern, rational). Folklorist Sabina Magliocco provides an excellent overview of this historical context, and notes the more recent shift to culturally relative definitions of religion that emphasize the connection between the human and the divine, and the importance of a cohesive moral/symbolic meaning-making system (and I'll note that Magliocco in particular has done really fascinating work on neo-paganism and Wicca as contemporary folk religions). So if religion encompasses many of these traits, what is folk religion?

One way of defining folk religion relies on contrast. Folklore pioneer of this topic Don Yoder defines folk religion as: "the totality of all those views and practices of religion that exist among the people apart from and alongside the strictly theological and liturgical forms of the official religion" (14).

However, starting from this point privileges monotheistic and codified religions. It implies that without a certain amount of institutionalization, religions aren't really religions. Magliocco comments on the role of Christianity in influencing this historical trend in scholarship:

> In both indigenous and peasant forms of religiosity, encounters with the divine could take very different forms from what was expected in Christian traditions. Too, the hierarchical organizational model common to many Christian faiths has often been taken to be the standard by which religions are defined, and those lacking centers of worship, holy writs, trained clergy and an established liturgy have been seen as less legitimate, or even deficient in the characteristics that define religion. (138)

In other words, because the bulk of religious scholarship in the West was happening in a Christian context, Christianity became the default religion by which all other religions were measured…and found wanting. Further, this view establishes a false dichotomy of official/unofficial religion. And as I've long pondered in regard to dualism and gender, it's rare to find dualism without hierarchy.

One of the contemporary and accepted definitions of the intersection of folklore and religion rebrands it as vernacular religion; vernacular basically means "everyday" if you're not familiar with the term, so vernacular language means everyday language or slang, how you might talk to your buddies and not your boss. Leonard Primiano is the one to suggest this term, and he defines it as: "religion as it is lived: as human beings encounter, understand, interpret, and practice it" (44).

This more inclusive definition ditches dualism and conceptual hierarchies. And it still lets folklorists access what we're interested in, and what we do best: the study of human creativity in informal transmission.

There are other places where religion and folklore intersect. Myth is an obvious one; so is ritual. The body art of religious folk groups is another area deserving of study, as are rite of passage, holiday, and foodways (each of which have both sacred and secular manifestations in many cultures. Then there are other minor genres like pilgrimages (perhaps a form of ostension?), prayers, curses, exorcisms, altars, and more.

So many folklore genres tie into religious belief and practice that one major takeaway is that spiritual/religious belief is a major part of many human societies, and is thus deserving of study. And we do good work when we take seriously the variations that naturally arise as part of expressive culture, rather than trying to squash them in the interests of presenting a united front. This is why it's important to have both insiders and outsiders of religious groups studying folk religion; we have different agendas, different biases, and different reasons for wanting to do this work. Insiders will often want to preserve the dignity of a religious practice, while outsiders won't face the same prohibitions on topics that are too close to home. Both come with pros and cons, so we need both.

In fact, the more woven into daily social life a given religious practice is, the more it's worthy of study. Family folklore, whether religious or not in nature, exemplifies this. The things that you "have always done that way" as part of your family's religious practice have deep links to enculturated beliefs about what is right, true, and good. These practices have likely patterned your worldview, and this is also why it's worth studying the practices of non-believers or atheists who have identified and rebelled against those strictures.

Then, of course, there are all the beliefs about gender, sex, and sexuality that accompany (folk) religion. An attempt at an exhaustive list would include what a given religious folk group believes about gender roles, contraception, abortion, sexual orientation, public vs. private sex acts, the proper relationship between sex and marriage (if any!), virginity, and more.

I could keep going, but I think I've made my point: that the informal religious beliefs and practices that comprise folk religion are worthy of study and understanding. We don't need to agree with them in order to study them, and in fact, an outsider may be more courageous in applying scholarly analytical techniques than a believer. As an atheist, I actually rather like the idea that we can understand humans better by studying their (perceived/believed) interactions with the divine; it doesn't require me to believe in the divine, but rather look at the sacred as a mirror that humans have been using for centuries if not millennia to see ourselves reflected in, and to guide us through the darkness of uncertain times.

References:

Magliocco, Sabina. "Religious Practice." *A Companion to Folklore,* edited by Regina F. Bendix and Galit Hasan-Rokem, Blackwell Publishing Ltd, 2012, 136-153.

Primiano, Leonard Norman. "Vernacular Religion and the Search for Method in Religious Folklife." *Western Folklore* vol. 54, no. 1, 1995, pp. 37-56.

Yoder, Don. "Toward a Definition of Folk Religion." *Western Folklore* vol. 33, no. 1, 1974, pp. 2-15.

HOLIDAY

Holidays are a folklore genre that span multiple modes of transmission: verbal, customary, and material (though I've intentionally inserted this chapter amidst the customary folklore genres section of this book, since holidays feel very custom-adjacent to me).

We can broadly define holidays as special celebratory days within a culture's calendrical/seasonal cycle that may have both secular and sacred components, or may focus more on one or the other. Some holidays have religious connections, while others do not. But all holidays have regional and temporal variations, and analyzing those variations interacting with tradition is what makes them interesting to folklorists.

Jack Santino, one of the folklorists who's extensively studied holidays, describes them as having many components:

> certain foods and beverages (as well as the act of feasting), music, noise (as distinct from music –

> firecrackers, for instance, or the popping of the cork on a champagne bottle), costuming, masking, parading, dancing, playing games and watching them, decorating, and performing religious rituals specific to the holidays, such as going to midnight mass at Christmas or to temple at Yom Kippur. (13)

Ritual, as Santino notes, plays a large role in holiday celebrations. These repeated, symbolic actions may or may not have religious connotations; I'd argue that trick-or-treating is just as much of a ritual as going to Mass. Rituals might be specific to families and thus part of their family folklore, or they might be shared by entire national or ethnic or religious folk groups.

Going into a bit more detail about the connection between holiday and ritual, Martha Sims and Martine Stephens write:

> Seasonal celebrations also often combine sacred and secular features. Springtime celebrations of renewal, for example, are not only indications of significant beliefs within a particular religion's practice. Formal sacred rituals surrounding seasonal holidays may happen in places of worship; however, in members' homes, informal, more secularized rituals may also occur, marking the date as personally significant to the member as well as significant to the entire congregation of their church or religious group. Such distinctions take the holiday to a new level, allowing members to make their commitment and belief more personal, more integral to their own daily lives in addition to part of a larger

> system with which they may have only weekly (or sometimes less frequent) contact. For some, this personal or more distinctly family or community-based ritual may involve a special food that grandmother cooks only on that holiday, or a special family event, like getting up early on the day after Christmas to go shopping. (104)

In other words, the rituals associated with holidays bounce between formal and informal manifestations. They can be high- or low-commitment in terms of time, energy, and money. Some are extremely personal, while others can be shared with entire communities.

Many holidays have their roots in ancient festivals, whether devoted to the worship of deities or the turning of the seasons (like solstices). However, whenever the concept of invented traditions comes up, we folklorists talk about how origins are not always relevant to why and how holidays are celebrated today. If you've got the data to make assertions about the past, cool; if not, focus on the present. Remember, folklore always serves multiple functions/purposes, so if a holiday's not serving the people who celebrate it, it'll drop out of circulation.

Take, for example, Halloween. While tracing its exact origins is challenging, we know that it formerly had associations with the dead, and was thought of as the night when the veil between the lands of the living and the dead grew thin. As Linda S. Watts notes in the *Encyclopedia of American Folklore*, "The origins of Halloween are probably in the Celtic Day of the Dead or festival of Samhain, an occasion that marks summer's end and the arrival of a new pagan year" (187). These probable origins may explain some of the ghostly and grim imagery that appears at Halloween, though again, I'm hesitant to commit too much to this kind of overarching explanation.

One thing we can fruitfully observe, however, is the gradual shift from Halloween being a past-oriented holiday to a future-oriented holiday. Alan Dundes hypothesizes that American folklore reflects the wide-ranging American world-view (or belief system/paradigm) that favors looking to the future rather than the past, and this is found in our holidays and other realms of expressive culture too.

Dundes writes:

> Americans have reworked many old world cultural elements and predictably enough, the American versions of customs with European cognates reveal the unmistakable influence of future orientation. For example, in the celebration of All Souls Day in Europe, respect is paid to the dead, that is, to the ancestors, to the past. (The same is true of All Saints Day inasmuch as saints are part of the past.) In the United States, the Halloween festival has been converted to a celebration for children, not parents. Though remains of departed spirits survive in the form of ghosts and other creatures, memorial visits to the graves of ancestors have been replaced by parents giving treats to children who threaten to play pranks on them. In accordance with a futuristic-optimistic view, the child – which represents the future – is bribed to be good. The emphasis is upon the child, the future, rather than upon the deceased ancestor. (64-65)

Watts corroborates this: "it is children rather than demons that Halloween tries to appease" (187).

We see other facets of contemporary American culture in Halloween as well: gender and ethnic stereotypes appear in costumes, and legends play with our beliefs in predatory behavior, both realistic and supernatural (for instance, the contemporary legend about the person putting razor blades in apples or psychedelic drugs in candy to hand out to trick-or-treaters). Commercialization, of course, is rampant.

Still, Halloween as a folk holiday persists, with local interpretations of how to celebrate it informing people's experiences of it. As folklorists, this is what we're after: the variations upon tradition that showcase different facets of identity and culture. And, of course, holidays are often fun to engage with, as participants and scholars alike!

References:

Dundes, Alan. Thinking Ahead: A Folkloristic Reflection of the Future Orientation in American Worldview. *Anthropological Quarterly* vol. 42, no. 2, 1969, pp. 53-72.

Santino, Jack. *All Around the Year: Holidays and Celebrations in American Life*. University of Illinois Press, 1994.

Sims, Martha C., and Martine Stephens. *Living Folklore: An Introduction to the Study of People and Their Traditions*. Utah State University Press, 2005.

Watts, Linda S. *Encyclopedia of American Folklore.* Infobase Publishing, 2007.

FOLK MEDICINE

If you've gargled with salt water to cure a sore throat or eaten ginger for an upset stomach, you've engaged in folk medicine.

In folklore studies, we define folk medicine as the traditional cures and remedies of a folk group. As with many genres of folklore, the genre name is meant to reflect how the material is transmitted informally, not to be a statement on its truth value, scientific rigor, or lack thereof (and no, it's just not herbal remedies). I'll dive into some of these issues in this chapter.

Folk medicine straddles the areas of customary folklore and material culture; it's a form of traditional behavior inflected by belief, but also often carries over into the physical realm, as expressed in medicines, ritual objects, and diseased/diagnosed bodies. So while we consider it to be its own genre of folklore, it can take different forms (physical, behavioral, belief-based) depending on how it's manifesting in a given context.

It's important to note that folk medicine can coexist with modern/biomedical medicine; the two are not mutually opposed or exclusive. It can involve modern medical cures and technologies, but the key difference is that it's not typically endorsed by institutional medical figures. However, because there are different levels of authority in groups that may or may not be institutional in nature, it's important to note that folk medicine can still come from an authority figure, such as a ritual or religious expert who nonetheless does not hold a title or position in an institution.

While folk medicine tends not to come from doctors, there are of course exceptions. One time in grad school I had a terrible cough, and a doctor at the student health center advised that I gargle with cough syrup. Because that's an off-label use of a biomedical product, I count it as an instance of folk medicine.

We might also look at what doctors and nurses do in their own lives, outside of professional contexts. As an occupational folk group, medical professionals have their own folklore, which David Hufford has brilliantly chronicled. But when doctors and nurses go home and tend to sick family members, what do *they* do? Do they advise sick kids to gargle with salt water, or what? This is an area that deserves more research.

In terms of classification, we often consider folk medicine to be a subset of folk belief/superstition, and catalog it according to the Wayland D. Hand system of classification (at least, that's what we did in the UC Berkeley Folklore Archive; I can't speak to the cataloguing systems of other folklore archives). There's a bit of a continuum between folk medicine and folk religion, too, as religious folk groups often have their own healing customs that hook into religious belief about what causes illness (demonic possession, spirit possession, etc.).

Remedies for different ailments often follow similar logic, and this is where sympathetic magic comes in. We've observed a number of remedies – such as those for wart cures – that involve using contagious magic or sympathetic magic to try to banish the offending feature.

When I teach folk medicine in the college classroom, I often have students collect texts (like individual remedies) from each other, asking about the following:

- Headaches
- Allergies
- Sore throats / colds
- Hiccups
- Hangovers / upset stomachs
- Skin conditions (acne, warts)

I've observed that wart cures seem to be on the decline in younger folk groups, while cold and hiccup cures are going strong. Could just be the folk groups I'm teaching, but I get the sense that the more mysterious and incurable a condition seems, the more likely that folk medicine will cluster around it. Also hangover cures tend to be popular among American college students, and I'm curious about the degree to which this might be a cross-cultural thing.

The subject of complementary and alternative medicine is a contentious one in some circles, but remember: folklorists don't necessarily care whether certain cures are efficacious. Rather, we're interested in the insights that studying folk medicine can provide into social groups and worldview. If you're interested in this topic, I highly recommend the book

Healing Logics edited by folklorist Erika Brady, which you can find online as well as in print. The book's overview reads:

> Scholars in folklore and anthropology are more directly involved in various aspects of medicine – such as medical education, clinical pastoral care, and negotiation of transcultural issues – than ever before. Old models of investigation that artificially isolated "folk medicine," "complementary and alternative medicine," and "biomedicine" as mutually exclusive have proven too limited in exploring the real-life complexities of health belief systems as they observably exist and are applied by contemporary Americans. Recent research strongly suggests that individuals construct their health belief systems from diverse sources of authority, including community and ethnic tradition, education, spiritual beliefs, personal experience, the influence of popular media, and perception of the goals and means of formal medicine. *Healing Logics* explores the diversity of these belief systems and how they interact – in competing, conflicting, and sometimes remarkably congruent ways. This book contains essays by leading scholars in the field and a comprehensive bibliography of folklore and medicine.[1]

There are a number of areas where folk medicine intersects with gender and sexuality, too, which I don't have space to get into here in depth, but they include how menstruation is regarded and treated, how pregnancy is handled (including midwifery practices), and the more general area of sex education, when it's done non-institutionally (learning about sex and relationships through friends, family, and peer groups).

And, given that I'm revising this chapter during a global pandemic, I'll briefly mention that folk medicine tends to be heightened in times of uncertainty or in response to conditions that are not well understood. *stares at former president's recommendation to inject bleach to combat the coronavirus*

By studying folk medicine, we can attend to the complex relationships between bodies, groups, and beliefs. This is yet another genre of folklore that pretty much everyone has engaged with at some point in their lives, consciously or not, whether this knowledge is held in high regard or low. So we'd do well as scholars of expressive culture to have it on our radar, regardless of whether a tickle in our throats sends us rushing for salt water to gargle with or not!

References:

Brunvand, Jan Harold. *The Study of American Folklore: An Introduction*. Fourth edition. W. W. Norton & Company, 1998 [1968, 1978, 1986].

Hufford, David. "Customary Observances in Modern Medicine." *Western Folklore* vol. 48, no. 2, 1989, pp. 129-143.

FOODWAYS

Every individual needs to eat to survive, and thus every culture has its food traditions (a.k.a. foodways). But folklorists are interested in food for a ton of reasons, including the role of tradition and variation and the display of identity.

Folklorists define foodways as the study of culture through food. We're specifically interested in those foods that are transmitted folklorically: foods that are passed along through informal and traditional means. We study the preparation, selection, consumption, and preservation of foods, ranging from recipes and meal assembly to the norms and rituals governing consumption.

Is it considered polite or impolite to eat with your hands? What are the "correct" sides to go with your plate of BBQ? Which foods should never, ever appear on the same plate together? Which foods go on an altar to ancestors or deities? How did Cincinnati chili evolve? Folklorists studying foodways answer these questions, and more!

While we consider foodways to be an area of material

culture – the physical manifestation of folklore – food weaves in and out of other kinds of folklore. Timothy Lloyd documents the folk speech associated with Cincinnati chili in terms of how you order it (asking for a "five-way no onions" for example). There are urban legends about the deliberate contamination of fast food by disgruntled workers (Kentucky Fried Rat, anyone?). Food appears as a theme in other folk narrative genres too; think of folktales and fairy tales about gingerbread men and houses, or wolves devouring little girls. We could study the occupational folklore of food service workers, whether they're in fast food or fancy restaurants. And so on.

But since food exists on the physical plane, we use a lot of the same techniques to document it as we would body art, vernacular architecture, and so on. We ask about the process and materials involved in making it. Who buys the groceries or raises the crops? How are foods sorted and organized in storage? When something's not going to be eaten right away, how is it preserved for later? A lot of these processes are folkloric in nature, in that they're passed along through informal channels of transmission. Many people's interactions with food are learned in the natal home, leading to a "well, that's just how we've always done it" attitude, which is always a sign that there's folklore at work.

Folklorists who study food collect recipe texts, but also consider entire meals to be "texts" that we would document and study. We want to know the techniques that go along with dishes and meals, as well as the less-tangible aspects of how foods are grouped together, why certain foods are chosen over others, and so on.

A major area of food study involves documenting holiday foods. The food associated with special occasions tend to have a unique significance in people's emotional lives, and to be fiercely upheld and guarded. Similarly, the foods that come from your family's folklore – what *your* family eats on Christmas morning, or does for birthdays – tend to be near and dear to people's memories.

With Thanksgiving being on my mind while writing the original blog post this chapter was based on, I'd also point out that food helps illustrate tradition and variation in concrete ways. In most parts of America, the turkey is the centerpiece of the Thanksgiving meal, with a handful of "necessary" sides (mashed potatoes, gravy, and stuffing). These represent what is traditional (or stable) about the Thanksgiving meal. From there, variation becomes apparent: what about sweet potatoes, green beans, corn casserole? Are pies a necessity? How much of the variation is governed by regional, ethnic, or religious identity? What if you're vegetarian? And so on.

Food fulfills multiple functions in people's lives. Obviously the first is physical nourishment, but beyond that, food helps build shared identity. Many of us have go-to comfort foods that we eat when we're feeling down, and often these are reminiscent of foods that we were fed while ailing youngsters. Food thus has an emotional impact for many people.

Food is also linked with religious belief and behavior for many; food prohibitions exist for entire food groups, or on certain days of feasting or fasting. The audience for foodways is not always human, as some people interact with the divine through ritual sacrifice, altar offerings, and so on. Bizarrely, my Jewish-but-not-religiously-so upbringing influenced my food tastes quite a bit, such that I don't really like pork, even though we never kept Kosher.

Sometimes foodways and ethnicity are closely interlinked. When you think of foods by ethnic category – Indian food, Italian food, and so on – you're thinking of how that culture's foodways have been consolidated and repackaged for consumers. That represents a homogenizing process; having been to India, I know that the food from Indian restaurants in America represents only a narrow slice of the foods actually eaten in various parts of India. The stereotypes and slurs thrown at various groups can involve food, too.

Other times, regional identity governs foodways more than ethnic identity. As Martha Sims and Martine Stephens remind us:

> Consider New Year's Day food traditions of different communities in the United States. Midwesterners often celebrate with sauerkraut and pork for luck, traditions that have been brought to the U.S. by the Germans who settled in Pennsylvania, Ohio, and Indiana. Southerners may celebrate with blackeyed peas and other foods that have come from southern agriculture, and some Texans eat tamales on New Year's Day. Not all the people who follow these traditions may be of German or Mexican descent or originally from the South, but because the people who live around them eat these kinds of foods, they do, too. The tradition is no longer associated with a particular ethnic or national group, but with a local, geographically bounded group. (38-39)

I'd be remiss if I didn't mention gender identity in relation to food. In many cultures, the emotional labor expected of women extends to food preparation, acquisition, preservation, and clean-up. Certain foods are regarded as more suitable for men or women in America at least; the unspoken norms governing what it's okay to eat on a first date, or who should have beer vs. wine, or a burger vs. a salad, are quite prevalent.

And as a body scholar, I'm always interested in the physical nature of our relationships with food: how food feels settling in our bodies, what we think of as "healthy" food, and so on. The issue of access to health food is a systemic one, impacting how we think of social class, fatness, and stigma.

I love food, so I could go on and on about it. For now, though, I'm curious: if you're an American reader, what are your family's Thanksgiving food traditions? And if you're not American, what have your experiences of Thanksgiving been (perhaps ranging from seeing it represented on American TV shows to being invited to spend the holiday with an American family; when I lived in Estonia, I did my best to put on a Thanksgiving meal that I could invite my colleagues to)?

References:

Lloyd, Timothy. "The Cincinnati Chili Culinary Complex." *Western Folklore* vol. 40, no. 1, 1981, pp. 28-40.

Sims, Martha C., and Martine Stephens. *Living Folklore: An Introduction to the Study of People and Their Traditions*. Utah State University Press, 2005.

BODY ART

Body Art is a classic genre of folklore that is often overlooked as trivial, or perceived as something that shouldn't/doesn't count as folklore because it's somehow simultaneously too mundane and too popular.

See, I've worked pretty hard to refute the notion that folklore is "just" fairy tales, myths, and legends... but even once people wrap their heads around that, they often tend to stick to defining folklore as primarily verbal. And there *are* many well-known genres of folklore that are performed and transmitted verbally: jokes, riddles, proverbs, slang/folk speech, and so on. So it's not unreasonable to think of "folklore" and leap straight to the verbal stuff.

However, folklore also exists in customary and physical forms. Material culture, the physical manifestation of folklore, is found in all societies, because all humans share the same basic physical needs (for food, shelter, and clothing), and they meet these needs in ways that are patterned by both tradition and variation. Body art is a genre belonging to the category of material culture, and we define it in folklore studies as any intentional aesthetic supplementation to or modification of the body.

I get this definition from Dr. Pravina Shukla's book *The Grace of the Four Moons,* which has influenced how I think about the self as the first audience, before one even steps outside. For all that Shukla's book is an ethnography of women's daily dress in India, it's important to consider how these concepts apply close to home.

As I state in a blog post discussing how I implement these ideas in the classroom:

> A lot of students came to my body art class expecting to spend the whole semester talking about tattoos and other permanent or extreme body mods. We will certainly discuss those things, but I'm also trying to give my students vocabulary and concepts for studying the daily clothing choices that surround them. I'm assigning a handful of fieldwork projects, for example, that could include looking at tattoos and piercings, but will mostly be about observing the clothing of people around them. I like to think that I'm giving them tools to critically interpret the visual culture of clothing, in order to perhaps be a bit more savvy about brands and advertising and the commodification of bodies.[1]

So, no, body art isn't just about tattoos and other major body mods. We study daily dress as well as special occasion attire; costumes, uniforms, and nudity; hair (on your head, facial, grooming in general) and makeup; jewelry; and body shaping technologies, from corsets and footbinding to dieting and bodybuilding.

Body art is important to study because it showcases social hierarchies, economic stratification, religious identity, and gender, among other things. Our bodies are at once very intimate and personal, and very public and visible.

Many societies, for instance, differentiate between how people of a certain gender should dress and groom their bodies, despite the fact that sexual dimorphism in humans (the physical differences between adult male and females, to briefly be very binary about it) is pretty minimal, compared to other species of mammals. In India, where I've traveled, as well as studied from Shukla's book, women's daily dress maps where they are in their life cycle (single? married? with children or not? widowed?) as well as portraying important aspects of their heritage (religion, region of origin, ethnicity, caste). In the U.S., women's bodies are increasingly held to unrealistically narrow beauty standards, with economic class and race being major structuring elements of which beauty technologies women will have access to in order to be slimmer, tanner, more symmetrically featured. At the same time, beauty subcultures have proliferated, with more trends and styles than ever to choose from.

In Shukla's words, gender is a core structuring element of body art, and this is especially true of religious body art:

> [T]he study of body art regularly shows how religious identity is expressed through clothes, hairstyle, and accessories – a *burqa*, side locks, or a *yarmulke* – and the absence or presence of certain ornaments, such as a pendant depicting Jesus on a cross, or a flash of red

> *sindur* on the hair part. Specialized apparel indicates differences of religion and culture to others, and also to the self. The Hasidic Jewish community distinguishes itself by specialized clothing for each gender: the men in large black hats, black kaftans, beards, and side locks (*peyes*), and the women in long-sleeved dresses, wearing either turbans or wigs (*sheitel*), since they are not supposed to show their hair in public. Someone passing by will recognize these people as orthodox Jews, and members of their community will be able to tell, by specifics of dress alone, which of the six social classes of Hasidic Jews somebody belongs to; the people so dressed will be reminded by their clothing of their responsibilities in behavior. (419)

Shukla goes on to discuss the daily dress of Pentecostals, Amish, and Mormons, alongside the dress of Muslims and Jews which, in the context of North America, often has a political connotation.

I'd add that a major body modification – circumcision – with religious components has become both mainstream and quite controversial in recent years in the U.S. Activists point to an infant's lack of ability to consent to this surgical procedure being done on their bodies, as well as how it interferes with sexual functioning (which has always been a claim regarding female genital cutting). In the U.S., male circumcision is not done for religious purposes per se, but rather became popular in the last century due to an anti-masturbation campaign that's largely been forgotten today. And yet, in other countries and cultures and eras, it remains a marker of religious identity.

By providing you with a definition of body art and some

key examples of how it expresses identities such as gender and religion, I hope I've given you some food for thought. If we all engage in this form of folklore daily, sometimes with more reflection and sometimes with less, what does it mean when we focus on it, on the traditions and variations we enact on our skin, hair, and faces? How are we expressing our various identities, or alternately concealing them? And how does this awareness enhance our knowledge of the cultural spheres we're constantly navigating?

References:

Shukla, Pravina. *The Grace of Four Moons: Dress, Adornment, and the Art of the Body in Modern India.* Indiana University Press, 2008.

FOLK ART

IF YOU'VE MADE friendship bracelets or mailbox stands from scratch, guess what, you've participated in folk art. It's a global and significant human activity.

One of the main areas of material culture that folklorists study – and that the public associates with our field – is folk art. We tend to use folk art and folk craft interchangeably, though they have slightly different connotations. Art tends to imply visual excellence, while craft connotes functionality, daily use, and mundane contexts.

Jan Brunvand writes that folk crafts "are usually thought of as amateur labor resulting in traditional homemade objects that are primarily functional" (544) whereas "folk art is usually thought of as the purely decorative or representational items produced by traditional means" (547). The two obviously overlap, though, which is a major reason we study them as a continuum. One person's art might be another's craft and all that.

Henry Glassie, one of the preeminent scholars of folk art, reminds us that such categories are relative:

> When a view from within a tradition is adopted, art separates from other activities, good art separates from bad art, but nothing separates folk and other art. Distinctions arise when we view the art of one tradition from the perspective of another. When that is done, it seems as though one's own tradition produces art, while the tradition of the other produces folk art. (271)

Lynne McNeill frames this discussion more in terms of what makes something a folk object, highlighting its patterns of use and circulation rather than its origin (having a folk context of creation still counts, but relying on it as the only trait we're interested in significantly narrows what we'd study as material culture and folk art in particular). From there, she discusses friendship bracelets as an example of folk art, which a student might hypothetically collect from their sister:

There's obviously a pattern of creation: this object is handmade, using a technique that your sister learned from her friends on the swim team, and this individual bracelet, like all the others she's made, uses a common and easy-to-produce design that your sister has enhanced with her own creative embellishments and color choices. Other girls on the swim team make similar, but not identical, bracelets on a regular basis. There's tradition in the style and technique, and variation in the color choices and unique patterns of knots. Clearly a folk object. (53-54)

In addition to examples from children's folklore like friendship bracelets and fortune tellers or cootie catchers, other types of folk art include quilting, basket-making, pottery, mailbox stands, accessories for hunting or agriculture like cattle guards and fencing types, wood-carving, rag rug weaving, spinning, knitting and crocheting, dyeing, blacksmithing, carpentry, barrel-making, and more. There are as many examples as there are ways for people to engage with tradition in their daily lives, though some genres are more widespread than others (e.g., most cultures develop a way to store and carry things whereas scrapbooking is pretty uniquely contemporary due to the availability of supplies for it). And there's often a gendered dimension to this work, with some of the lower-status crafts relegated to women (which I discuss a bit in the chapter on women's folklore.

In the larger art world, folk artists are sometimes thought of as outsider artists, self-trained artists, and so on. But due to how folklorists are oriented towards culture and group identity, we're fond of reminding others that art never happens in a vacuum, no matter how high-art it might be considered. John Vlach, a major scholar of material culture, writes:

> No genuine folk artist can ever be completely self-taught. Certainly folk artists may work alone, even in seclusion, but they will work within a socially sanctioned set of rules for artistic production which they expect will insure the acceptability of their completed pieces. Thus they are mentally connected even if physically isolated (quoted in Brunvand, 551).

So, clearly folklorists approach the idea of art a bit differently than people with training in fine arts. While we may interview individuals in our fieldwork, we always study the individual within the context of tradition. And we like to think that we do so without the elitist lens that some fine-arts-oriented people apply, judging the merit of the artistic technique rather than engaging with it in a broader cultural context.

I'll close with another Glassie quote, and encourage you to read his work if you want to know more about the study of folk art:

> But if we wish to learn what art is, if we wish to understand the things we call folk art for themselves and not as ciphers in the small system of our consciousness, then folk art demands a different context, not a context conditioned by Kandinsky and Picasso and shaped by dealers and scholars, but a context constructed by the people who made the art. In its own context, when the weaver sits at her loom, when the supplicant touches his forehead to the prayer rug, folk art is not a corollary or critique of modern art, it is a part of the experience of life. At life's center, in the midst of common work, people have always found and always will find ways to create things that simultaneously enfold themselves, present their social affinities, and mutter about the enormity of the universe. In that context these things are not folk art. They are art. (273-274)

References:

Brunvand, Jan Harold. *The Study of American Folklore: An Introduction*. Fourth edition. W. W. Norton & Company, 1998 [1968, 1978, 1986].

Glassie, Henry. "The Idea of Folk Art." *Folk Art and Art Worlds,* edited by John Vlach and Simon Bronner, U. M. I. Research Press, 1992, 269-274.

McNeill, Lynne S. *Folklore Rules: A Fun, Quick, and Useful Introduction to the Field of Academic Folklore Studies*. Utah State University Press, 2013.

SPECIAL TOPICS

WOMEN'S FOLKLORE

Studying folklore by genre is pretty well established, though that's not the only way to go about it. It's also common to study folklore by geographical region and time period, for example. And studying the folklore of a single folk group is also one way to go. As such, we also consider women's folklore to be a major topic in the field. But it didn't used to be that way.

Folklore is equal-opportunity, right? Anyone can become an active bearer of any genre, and perform it to their heart's content, whether we're talking about jokes, rituals, or traditional recipes, right?

Well, no. Many genres of folklore are considered appropriate for one gender alone, and further, over the past few centuries folklorists have gravitated toward more masculine and public genres. This default orientation has been called out and corrected in the last few decades, leading to the study of what we now call women's folklore.

Studying women's folklore means focusing on women as a folk group: examining the shared culture, traditions, narratives, beliefs, and behavior that women transmit and perform with/for one another. However, this is also necessarily an intersectional enterprise (though I have to note that intersectionality is a concept folklorists are late and few to adopt), because gender identity is always situated within other identities. Gender is not a monolithic identity; it is always inflected by other factors. Plus folklorists are usually anti-essentialist, preferring not to reduce the totality of a person to one facet of their identity. So we might study the folklore of Jewish women, or African-American women, or middle-class immigrant women, or lesbian women, and so on.

As with children's folklore and occupational folklore (covered in another few chapters), women's folklore encompasses many genres and functions, and changes significantly over time and space. Domestic, private, and household contexts generate different types of folklore than do public and commercial ones… which also impacts what folklore scholars have access to. If a male scholar goes to do fieldwork in a society where men dominate public spaces and it'd be inappropriate for him to sit alone with a bunch of women to collect their folklore, guess what he's going to end up collecting? That's right, more men's folklore than women's folklore. Hopefully he has the sense not to pass it off as the folklore of *all* people in XYZ culture.

When I teach women's folklore, I like to focus on a few different aspects: images/representations of women in folklore, genres of folklore associated with and practiced by women, and feminist ethnography. In my mind, it's valuable to foreground gender as a major theme in most folklore, and this is a useful place to start since many students can leap into the study of, say, fairy tales, and recognize the highly dualistic ways in which female and male characters are portrayed. Adding contextual information about who the tellers, writers, and collectors are can further help us understand how folktales are a women's art form in many cultures, which leads into the study of women's folklore genres, and in turn helps us think about ethical and feminist ways of collecting and studying folklore.

Folklorists have also developed the theoretical concept of coding (covered in more detail in the next chapter) in close connection with women's folklore. Put briefly, since women as a distinct folk group lack power in many societies, we often come up with ways to disguise and downplay subversive messages.

As mentioned above, the study of women's folklore initially emerged as a corrective impulse. The first publication on the topic was *Women and Folklore: Images and Genres*, a collection of essays edited by Claire R. Farrer in 1975. In it, she observes: "We were stating that women's lives were not simply derivative and reproductive but were strongly active and productive. Our papers indicated as well that women's folklore was often responsive to a different aesthetic than the male pattern that ruled" (ix).

The question of aesthetics is an important one, and one that feminists in other fields have raised, investigating topics like women's writing and visual art. Many scholars of women's folklore are themselves women, and self-identified feminists, but not all. In some cases, women scholars were better positioned to access these topics than their masculine peers, with subjects like family stories and gossip, or narratives related to motherhood.

The field of women's folklore continued to expand, with

the 1985 publication of *Women's Folklore, Women's Culture* (edited by Rosan A. Jordan and Susan J. Kalčik), and the 1993 publications of *Feminist Messages: Coding in Women's Folk Culture* (edited by Joan N. Radner) and *Feminist Theory and the Study of Folklore* (edited by Susan Tower Hollis, Linda Pershing, and M. Jane Young). I regularly teach essays from all of these books, and the topics therein range from girls' playground games and quilting to images of women in fairy tales and religious texts. Some of my favorite essays document images of femininity in order to analyze and critique them, while others bring lesser-known women's folklore to light, such as traditional midwifery practice around the world.

The field of fairy-tale studies in particular has much in common with the study of women's folklore and the use of feminist theory as part of the analytical toolkit. Both fairy-tale retelling authors (Angela Carter, Anne Sexton, and Emma Donoghue for example) and fairy-tale scholars (Donald Haase, Anne Duggan, Jack Zipes, and Cristina Bacchilega stand out in my mind) have made gender, and femininity in particular, a focal point of their work. Fairy tales and other genres like gossip and folk medicine, often traditionally associated with women and hence denigrated as trivial or marginal, are thus receiving a lot of creative and critical attention right now, which I think is overdue.

We miss a lot when we assume that the traditional knowledge, behavior, stories, and material culture of the more visible or dominant gender is the extent of what that culture has to offer. Women's folklore offers a significant corrective to this assumption, and further, investigating the representations and replication of gender roles in traditional culture helps us better understand gender in general. I'm happy to say that the study of women's folklore is still going strong.

References:

Farrer, Claire R., ed. *Women and Folklore: Images and Genres.* Waveland Press, Inc., 1986 [1975].

CODING

No, I don't mean computer coding, but rather coding on a cultural level. If you've heard of the hanky code you know what I'm talking about...if you haven't, read on to learn about a folkloric phenomenon that exists to protect its participants!

All folklore is meaningful and transmits cultural messages. That's part of what we mean when we say folklore is a performance, or that folklore serves multiple functions. Bringing in the concept of coding means that we're specifically attuned to the messages that are coded in order to protect the people sending and receiving them.

As Joan Radner and Susan Lanser write in their groundbreaking essay on the topic, coding means:

> a set of signals–words, forms, behaviors, signifiers of some kind–that protect the creator from the consequences of openly expressing particular

> messages…the expression of transmission of messages potentially accessible to a (bicultural) community under the very eyes of the dominant community for whom these same messages are either inaccessible or inadmissible. (3)

The idea of people being bicultural is reminiscent of the concept of folk groups, which are always multiple and overlapping. The members of a national folk group (say, Americans) might all have some awareness of mainstream norms and values, while the members of a smaller folk group within that folk group (such as a sexual minority) would have the additional awareness that their very existence puts them at risk for retaliation from some.

Coding implies risk and danger of varying degrees. Among their examples, Radner and Lanser mention Civil War era enslaved people who used cryptic language to talk about how the Union army was doing, for fear of being punished or even killed if they were discovered to be interested in the topic; children's use of secret languages such as Pig Latin; and code-switching between languages among immigrants. These are all examples of folklore because they are informally transmitted cultural behaviors, whereas a military code might be something you learn from an institutional rather than a traditional source.

Certain codes are more, well, codified than others. The hanky code has been around for a few decades as a method for gay men to subtly advertise what kinds of sexual encounters they're looking for, and thus it's achieved a high degree of consistency and stability. As a protective mechanism, it can appear to the uninitiated that a man is just really fashionable…

not that he's advertising his sexual preferences. And again, to connect coding back to risk, homophobic crimes remain a reality, though perhaps less so than before. There are some places where it's still not safe to be openly gay.

Other kinds of coding are less obvious, and perhaps even less intentional. As Radner and Lanser note:

> We suggest that a context for implicit coding exists when there is a situation of oppression, dominance, or risk for a particular individual or identifiable group; when there is some kind of opposition in this situation that cannot safely be made explicit; and when there is a community of potential "listeners" from which one would want to protect oneself. (9)

Studying forms of culture that are subtle because they are meant to protect members of that culture is, obviously, difficult at times. Radner and Lanser suggest a number of coding strategies that scholars can identify, including:

- appropriation
- juxtaposition
- distraction
- indirection
- trivialization
- incompetence

It's important to note that coding isn't just limited to folklore; it can also occur in literature, the fine arts, and so on. Radner and Lanser note that this type of coding might look a little different, depending on complex issues of creativity, audience, production/transmission method, and so on. But they give a great example of how one coding strategy, incompetence, might appear in a literary context:

> In the eighteenth century, a woman writer's proclamation of literary incompetence in the preface was a conventional strategy by which the woman writer could say on her own behalf what she expected her audience to think: that she had little right to be writing and that her work was bound to be inferior. (22)

Similarly, we see many instances of coding in fairy tales, where female tellers and writers slip in gender-subversive messages that might go unnoticed because they take place in a fantastical setting. In this sense, coding is very much a feminist topic. But it speaks to the experiences of marginalized people everywhere, who creatively find ways to communicate about their situations while also evading notice and punishment from dominant groups.

References:

Radner, Joan, and Susan S. Lanser. "Strategies of Coding." *Feminist Messages: Coding in Women's Folk Culture,* edited by Joan Newlon Radner, University of Illinois Press, 1993, 1-29.

OCCUPATIONAL FOLKLORE

If you work a career that has you in contact with other humans, it's likely that you've been exposed to occupational folklore, or the informal traditions that accompany a career.

The definition I saw a while back on the New York Folklore Society's website[1] is one I like: "Occupational Folklore refers to the shared knowledge held by workers within a specific occupational group, as expressed through narrative arts, shared techniques and information, and through shared technology and hand-made objects."

While historically the focus of scholars of occupational folklore (or laborlore, as it's sometimes called) has been on old-timey, romanticized, and gendered occupations – the cowboy, the miner, the sailor – today we acknowledge that any profession potentially generates folklore that would be of interest to us. Folklorists have studied the lore of airline stewardesses, bartenders, retail workers, and homemakers too.

When we study occupational folklore, there are a few ways to approach it. Obviously we want to do fieldwork if we're able to, using participant-observation and interview techniques to obtain information from the workers. Sometimes we study laborlore according to the type of work involved, focusing on industrial jobs vs. rural jobs, crafting jobs vs. traveling jobs, and so on. Thus you might find studies of miners contrasting with studies of lumberjacks, or blacksmiths contrasted with factory workers.

Studies of occupational folklore might also emphasize the genres that dominate a given profession. Common genres found in the workplace include folk speech (often jargon used on the job); folk narrative (like personal narratives about an individual's experience, or legends about well-known characters in the profession); jokes and pranks; folk beliefs and stereotypes; customs or traditional behaviors (such as strategies for manufacturing items, or selling them); and body art (ranging from how people customize their uniforms to beliefs about what it's "appropriate" for people in a given profession to wear).

Labor unions occupy a significant place in occupational folklore studies. Archie Green was a folklorist who devoted his career to the study of occupational folklore, and among other things, he documented the songs of industrial workers and unions. Protest songs and work songs are a topic I haven't studied personally, but I know it's a pretty important one in the landscape of occupational folklore.

The workplace is an intriguing site of study for a couple of reasons. For one, often there's an institutional culture, a play-by-the-rules facet to work life, that isn't necessarily interesting to folklorists. We're not as into the formalized aspects of culture, but even in highly regimented workplaces, there are some breaths of informal culture and variation. Maybe the regulations or rules say to do things a certain way, but we've "always" been doing it this way, and thus new employees are inducted into the ranks of seasoned workers through a folkloric education process.

Gender, social class, and other identity markers also figure significantly into workplace culture. Some professions remain highly gendered; others are less so. Studying these shifts over time can give us insights into changing gender norms, for example, and where those intersect with other facets of identity. The concept of emotional labor is especially relevant here, as all jobs involve emotional labor of some sort (subsuming your feelings in the moment of being a professional is required of everyone), but those moments are often disproportionately distributed. In other words, women – especially women in service occupations – frequently face greater pressure to smile and be pleasant than men in similar positions.

My working hypothesis about why occupational folklore is so common especially in America goes beyond documenting the existence of workers as unique folk groups. I believe that economic inequality is simultaneously real and common, and yet also taboo as a topic. Sure, we can talk about it on the internet all day, but when we try to achieve reform, we bump into all sorts of obstacles. Belief in the American Dream, the pull-yourself-up-by-the-bootstraps meritocracy, remains strong. But when we share about labor experiences, we insert ourselves into the dilemmas of capitalism. We embody its contradictions. And thus, little by little, we contribute to the conversation, and possibly initiate change.

CHILDREN'S FOLKLORE

All adults have passed through childhood, which means we all have experience with children's folklore. The stuff is remarkably stable, and we're still figuring out why!

Like the categories of women's folklore and occupational folklore (covered in the previous chapters), children's folklore is an umbrella term that includes a large number of genres. What makes it children's folklore is the primary folk group involved in its transmission: children.

We find children's folklore across multiple modes of transmission, including all three of the main categories of folklore: verbal folklore, customary lore and belief, and material culture. Examples of verbal lore found among children include folk speech, jokes, and various narrative genres; examples of customary lore include superstitions like Bloody Mary, games (too many to list!), songs and rhymes (greasy grimy gopher guts, anyone?), and gestures (from greeting and leave-taking gestures to obscene ones); examples of material culture include crafts like making fortune tellers or origami, plus all the various ways kids interact with food and dress.

Oh, what's that, you don't know greasy grimy gopher guts? It's a popular American children's rhyme, and it totally exemplifies the variation inherent to folklore. Here are two texts:

- Great big globs of greasy, grimy gopher's guts / Mutilated monkey's meat / Little birdie's bloody feet / All whipped together in penetrated porpoise pus / And I forgot my spoon.
- Great big gobs of juicy, grimy gopher guts / Mutilated monkey feet, chopped-up parakeet / Eagle eyes in a great big bowl of pus / And me without a spoon.

In terms of how we study children's folklore, it's important to distinguish between folklore *by* children and folklore *for* children. The former is transmitted horizontally among members of a folk group or peer group without much in the way of hierarchy separating members from one another (which isn't to say that there's no hierarchy at work in groups of kids, but rather that it's not hierarchy based on age). The latter, folklore *for* children, is folklore that's transmitted vertically, from adults to kids. A prime example would be lullabies, a genre of folk song.

Similarly, it's important to distinguish children's folklore from children's literature. Folklore is usually characterized as informally transmitted traditional culture, which *might* occasionally take the form of the written word, whereas literature tends to be authored and more static, at least once it's published (yes, I know, there are always exceptions). So while we might see fairy tales as sometimes part of children's folklore in that kids retell fairy tales and play fairy-tale based games, we could also consider fairy tales to be children's literature, when they are authored by adults and presented to kids. Another notable disclaimer is that folklorists do not universally write children's books.

Children's folklore can provide a nice example of coding, too (or transmitting messages in a way so as to protect an oppressed or marginalized group from the consequences of their communication). Many children's folk groups have secret languages, such as Pig Latin in the U.S., which aren't all that terribly tough to decipher, but they give the illusion of privacy. Sometimes children do develop sophisticated ways of slipping things under the noses of adults, too; this can be for whimsical reasons, or for less-fun reasons (as when children are in situations of abuse and may be trying to communicate that to another adult or otherwise seek help).

As Lynne McNeill notes, children's folklore is an especially rich field of study precisely because of how children respond to and adapt concepts from the adult world:

> Children also have a ruthless sort of ranking system that emerges in their traditional games. Remember playing house? The selection process for who gets to be parents and who has to be kids (or pets!) is always interesting, as is the way in which roles are easily dismissed after being fought for. We can see in children's traditional games a reflection of their perception of adult life – the roles, the rules, and the social expectations into which they're going to have to assimilate at some point. The really cool

> thing is how those expectations are just as often obliterated by children's folklore as they are upheld. We grown-ups could probably learn something from that. (79)

Because I'm a history nerd, I'll briefly note that children's folklore became a significant field of study in the 19th century. Early children's folklore scholars tended to be British or American, but the study of children's folklore has spread across the world in the 20th century. Currently, there's a pretty big focus on how children interact with pop culture and the mass media.

This field has blossomed so much that I can't list every children's literature scholar here, but here are a few notable ones:

- William Wells Newell, American folklorist: *Games and Songs of American Children* (1883)
- Lady Alice Bertha Gomme, British folklorist: *The Traditional of England, Scotland, and Ireland: Tunes, Singing-Rhymes and Methods of Playing According to the Variants Extant and Recorded in Different Parts of the Kingdom* (1894-98)
- Peter and Iona Opie, British couple: *The Oxford Dictionary of Nursery Rhymes* (1952)

And here are a few major concepts:

- Newell's Paradox: children are both conservative and creative
- The triviality barrier: children's folklore ignored

because it is considered trivial

- The cultural construction of childhood (Philippe Ariès): the idea of childhood is a modern concept, was not culturally accepted until 17th century

Finally, why do we study children's folklore?

- Folklore teaches children about the world around them, so in studying their folklore, we learn what they learn
- Children are relatively powerless, but they gain and explore power through their folklore
- Among other functions, folklore provides children with an outlet for curiosity, rebellion, and exploring the arbitrary and authoritarian nature of the adult world

We could run through examples of children's folklore all day; when I teach this topic, it's generally one that most people can remember engaging with when younger (or currently, if there are children in their lives to observe and interact with).

Do you remember any folklore from your childhood?

References:

McNeill, Lynne S. *Folklore Rules: A Fun, Quick, and Useful Introduction to the Field of Academic Folklore Studies*. Utah State University Press, 2013.

FAMILY FOLKLORE

I love teaching units on family folklore because almost everyone can relate to it. Which sometimes leads to heated debates about the "right" foods to serve on Thanksgiving…!

Family folklore is often the first type of folklore that people encounter in their lives, and thus it can significantly shape how we experience culture. It's simultaneously complex and composite, with many tradition-bearers recalling and performing it. Here we'll dive into these concepts from a scholarly perspective.

In *Folklore: An Encyclopedia of Beliefs, Customs, Tales, Music, and Art, Volume 1,* family folklore is defined as:

> Traditional expressive behavior and its products that are transmitted by family members to family members and that pertain to relatives, family events, and family ways of being and doing. Family folklore includes stories, jokes, and songs about family members and events, as

> well as the ways relatives share those items with one another; festivals the family celebrates, such as religious and national holidays; foods, cooking instruction, ways of eating, and ways of gathering to eat within a family; family naming traditions; a family's ways of dancing; expressions and gestures a family uses; visual records of family life, such as arrangements of items inside and outside the home, photographs, photograph albums, videotapes, embroideries, and quilts; occupational, song, story, and craft traditions carried on within a family. (278-279)

In other words, family folklore encompasses many folklore genres. The common thread linking these otherwise distinct genres, whether verbal, customary, or material, is that:

- the family is the folk group transmitting this lore
- family is often the topic of the lore
- the family unit provides the context in which the lore is performed / maintained

While the content of any given family's lore is unique to them, many common themes emerge. American families often have narratives about ancestors who came over as immigrants, whether it happened recently or not. In *A Celebration of American Family Folklore,* the authors note that two major themes emerge in family stories: the character principle and the transition principle. The former refers to the tendency for stories about family members to evolve into character studies and to highlight personality traits of a given family member (which is also frequent in personal narratives). The latter designates the tendency to retain stories documenting a radical change in a family's history. Death and trauma are common themes here, as are stories of the lives of family members who are heroes, rogues, and survivors.

In terms of context, recall the distinction between active and passive bearers of folklore. Families tend to have many of each, sometimes with different people excelling at different genres. Here, of course, gender plays a role: many family food traditions are maintained by women, whereas occupational traditions might be maintained by the men of the family. As I've argued on my blog, the emotional labor[1] required for kin-keeping[2] is pretty gendered, and this dovetails with family folklore since a number of the activities required to do family relationship maintenance are folkloric in nature (organizing celebrations around holidays, keeping lists of who likes which foods and kinds of gifts, or coordinating holiday gift exchanges in large families all come to mind, as well as the connections between family lore and religious folklore that might govern holiday gatherings).

I've also mentioned that family folklore is composite in nature. You might get glimpses of a single event in the family's history refracted through a number of perspectives, with each rendition or telling (of, say, a family legend) acting like a puzzle piece, to be fit in with the rest before a coherent picture emerges. Sometimes certain people in a family "own" their stories or recipes, and choose who to pass them on to; sometimes this happens according to gender or perceived talent/interest; and sometimes people die before they pass on their traditions.

While I've given a handful of narrative examples here, verbal family folklore isn't limited to stories. Families often share folk speech with one another, from nicknames and naming traditions to slang words for food and ways of singing happy birthday (in my family, for example, my sister is known not as an overachiever but rather as an "over-a-cheeser" for reasons I don't have space to get into). When it comes to the American birthday song, my family has verbal folklore (such as add-ons after the standard birthday song ends) as well as customs (like my parents calling family members on their birthday to sing the birthday song over the phone, or in a voicemail message if the person doesn't pick up). Material traditions in families are also quite prevalent. Food is a favorite topic of many, but we shouldn't lose sight of material items ranging from heirlooms to crafts.

Family folklore is deeply related to worldview. Family narratives assert the shared identity of families; these stories help family members develop a shared sense of history, location, and roots. They can reveal where the family is in relation to the rest of the world: disengaged? intrepid explorers? saviors? victims?

Scholars of family folklore often run into the triviality barrier, or the assumption that this stuff is so everyday as to be uselessly mundane, so why bother studying it? The truth is that by studying the culture that unites – and sometimes divides – families, we gain valuable insights into the social glue of folklore, at the micro-cultural level of the family unit.

References:

Green, Thomas A., editor. *Folklore: An Encyclopedia of Beliefs, Customs, Tales, Music, and Art, Volume 1.* ABC-CLIO, 1993.

Zeitlin, Steve J., Amy J. Kotkin, and Holly Cutting Baker. *A Celebration of American Family Folklore: Tales and Traditions from the Smithsonian Collection*. Yellow Moon Press, 1982.

FOLKLORE AND DISABILITY

Folklore and disability interact in many ways, some upholding norms & some challenging them, but I would argue that understanding representations of disability in folklore can yield many insights into identity and power.

I decided to do a unit on disability, trauma, and mental health in fairy tales for my First Year Seminar students in the spring 2021 semester, and so of course while writing a draft of this chapter I'm knee-deep in research while trying to decide what to assign and what to teach. I've been researching the body in folklore for a while (at least since my dissertation on gender and the body in European fairy tales, published in 2012), and so it makes sense for me to also study disability in folklore. However, I didn't receive any instruction on this in grad school, which is kinda a bummer, so I'm doing what I can to rectify those gaps in my knowledge and get acquainted with disability studies on my own. Here's a bit of insight into my process.

First, some quick terms: I follow fairy-tale scholar Ann Schmiesing in describing disability as a broad umbrella term to include those with differences from an assumed "norm" (itself an unstable category!). Disabilities may be inborn or acquired, and it's a good reminder for those of us who are currently able-bodied that disability and trauma will come to us all eventually. Ableism refers to the "centering and dominance of nondisabled views and the marginalizing of disability" (Schmiesing 5) and it includes a bunch of problematic assumptions, such as "that all disabled people aspire to be an able-bodied norm, that disabled people are inferior to nondisabled people, and that disability defines and determines an individual's characteristics" (5).

We also have to keep in mind that contrasting the "normal" with the "abnormal" is a false dichotomy and a fairly recent game; in his introduction to *The Disability Studies Reader* Lennard J. Davis traces the intertwined history of industrialization and eugenics to place modern concepts of disability therein. He makes the point that "the association between what we would now call disability and criminal activity, mental incompetence, sexual license, and so on established a legacy that people with disabilities are still having trouble living down" (7). So these abstract categories and identity markers have very real impacts on people's lives.

Further, it's crucial to keep in mind that terms like "disability" and "disabled" are not unchanging constants. As the editors of *Disability in Different Cultures: Reflections on Local Concepts* describe in their introduction to the book:

> In exploring the wide variety of local concepts of and different ideas and beliefs about disability, it becomes

> strikingly clear just how differently a disability may be judged. In this light, *disability* can no longer be perceived as a physical, psychological or mental characteristic which a person is born with or has acquired in the course of her or his life. On the contrary, it becomes evident to what a large degree the attitudes and the interactions with others that are usual in the respective social context form and influence the nature and extent of a disability and thereby determine the life of the disabled person. This altered consciousness with regard to disabilities makes it possible to perceive a condition formerly held to be *natural* – where the disability was seen as an inborn physical state, entailing consequences viewed as inevitable – as something which can be both changed and shaped. (10, italics in original)

This is a great reminder that concepts of disability are not universal: yes, there are going to be some biological constants across time and space, but if a culture frames a different body as one with positive attributes, and moreover easily accommodates those differences, is it really the same as inhabiting a similar body in a culture that looks down on that body and refuses to accommodate its needs? The classic example here is visual impairment, which can technically be considered a disability, but since Western cultures accommodate those impairments with aids like contacts and glasses, would a person who wears glasses identify as disabled? Maybe, maybe not. This is also an issue that benefits from an intersectional gaze, or taking into account how multiple marginalizations might impact each other: a disability might be experienced way differently by someone who is rich vs. poor, white vs. a person of color (especially here in the U.S.), cis gender vs. trans gender, and so on.

Also, brief content note: I am going to mention and briefly describe some folklore texts that are potentially offensive, not to endorse them, but to analyze them. This is one of those reminders that folklore isn't all fairy tales and unicorns and puppies and sunshine; in cataloguing the whole range of traditional human expression and creativity, we're going to run into some nasty stuff.

One obvious point of overlap between folklore and disability is in the realm of folk speech. Slang and regional dialect all count as folk speech, and so you'll see slang terms for various types of disability. You'll also see folk similes, such as "as blind as a bat," to describe experiences of disability.

I actually grew up hyper-aware of folk speech around disability, because my mom taught special education for the bulk of her career. Hence I knew that calling someone a "retard" was a slur and therefore off the table. It boggles my mind to know that some people still use the word. Even words that are more generally regarded as not being slurs, such as "idiot" and "imbecile," have an unpalatable history of being used to describe people with developmental disorders a century ago, which ties into the history of eugenics. I try not to use ableist language, though it can be a struggle to find words to replace common phrases that most people don't view as problematic.

And – brief detour to a parallel here – of course language being political and/or problematized isn't universally agreed upon. I'm not heterosexual, and I'm in the camp of LGBTQ+ people who believe in reclaiming the word "queer." Some of us continue to view it as a slur, however, and choose not to self-identify that way. That's fine. As I understand it, the word "cripple," once seen as unfailingly negative, is being reclaimed by people in the disability community, imbuing "crip" with positive and communal associations, such as in the slogan "Crip the Vote" which I saw circulating in the last year. Since I'm not disabled, I'm not going to use that word to refer to someone else unless they say "yes, that's my preferred identification," same way as I'm not going to call someone "queer" unless they self-identify that way.

Disability shows up in a lot of folk narrative, too. Schmiesing, whose work I mention above, devotes her whole book to disability in the Grimms' fairy tales, and she makes use of fascinating analytical frames such as that of "narrative prosthesis," or the idea that in many narratives, the whole plot hinges around "fixing" the disability. We see this in fairy tales such as ATU 706, "The Maiden Without Hands." Also, there is a gorgeous French animated film version of this tale, *The Girl Without Hands* by Sébastien Laudenbach, which I cannot recommend highly enough; I haven't decided whether to teach it, in part because it's really really heavy).

Another classic example of disability in folk narrative is ATU 1317, "The Blind Men and the Elephant," though it's another example of a rather disparaging look at disabled people. The edited volume *Diagnosing Folklore: Perspectives on Disability, Health, and Trauma* also contains some examples of disability in folk narrative, such as the disfigured and deranged serial killers from urban legends in Diane Goldstein's essay and the personal narratives of traumatized war veterans in Kristiana Willsey's essay.

Disability is sometimes imbued with tinges of the supernatural, magic, and religion; recall the ancient Greek prophet Tiresias, who was struck blind by Hera (after a snake-induced transgender adventure) but rewarded with the gift of prophecy by Zeus. Or consider the changeling – a fairy child left with human parents, while the fairies raise the human child – which folklorists have argued may well have been a way to use the language of the fantastic to describe developmental disorders that were not yet understood.

However, many of these representations of disability in folklore are quite negative. I make the point in my review of Helen Oyeyemi's *Boy, Snow, Bird*[1] (while also ranting about how transphobic the book is) that turning a marginalized character (such as a disabled character) into a magical creature or a metaphor for something else is a crappy move: "to read disability as a metaphor for powerlessness is bullshit, in a culture where representation of disabled folks as themselves, as real people, is still lagging terribly."

So, this makes it tricky to simply say, "let's celebrate any/every instance of disability representation in folklore (or literature, or pop culture)." What if that representation is badly done, or inaccurate, or straight-up harmful? What if we (nondisabled folks) only see the "supercrip" (a.k.a. the overachiever, the person who "overcomes" their disability in an inspiration-porn kind of way) OR the disfigured villain (like Dr. Poison in the 2017 *Wonder Woman* film)? (side note: this is one reason I love the TV series *Avatar: The Last Airbender*, because I think they handle disability really well! Go Toph! also, my colleague Sara Cleto, who also writes about disability and folklore, has a blog post about disability in the show from the same creators, *The Dragon Prince*[2]).

I believe that folklorists can and should be doing work on disability. As Andrea Kitta and Trevor J. Blank point out in their introduction to *Diagnosing Folklore*: "One of the most significant problems with the study of stigma is that it tends not to take the lived experience of their affected by stigma into account and gives a voice instead to the medicalized authority and expert over lay knowledge" (7). Because attending to local and lay knowledge and prioritizing the voices of everyday people is basically the point of folklore studies, I am hoping that we can do this work, and do it well, though clearly those of us who are nondisabled need to examine our biases before undertaking such work.

Anyway, this is just a brief introduction to the intersections of disability and folklore; there are many more I haven't touched on here, in areas like material culture, customs, and more that I've heard of or read about but don't have a good enough command of to feel like I should include them here (for instance, the internet has allowed lots of disabled people to connect in unprecedented ways, so the folklore of the internet and social media would be one future area of study). Plus, as a nondisabled person, no doubt there are aspects to disabled culture(s) that I am missing, so I shouldn't speculate and risk misrepresenting them. Happy reading and thinking, everyone!

References:

Blank, Trevor J., and Andrea Kitta, editors. *Diagnosing Folklore: Perspectives on Disability, Health, and Trauma*. University Press of Mississippi, 2015.

Davis, Lennard J., editor. *The Disability Studies Reader. Fourth Edition.* Routledge, 2013.

Holzer, Brigitte, Arthur Vreede, and Gabriele Weigt, editors. *Disability in Different Cultures: Reflections on Local Concepts.* Transcript, 1999.

Schmiesing, Ann. *Disability, Deformity, and Disease in the Grimms' Fairy Tales*. Wayne State University Press, 2014.

FOLKLORE IN/AND LITERATURE

FOLKLORISTS DO MORE than collect folklore and analyze it; we also look for it in creative works that transform folklore into other kinds of culture, such as literature and/or pop culture. Fear not, there's a method to this madness.

We folklorists like to primly inform people that folklore is NOT literature: folklore is dynamic and ever-changing, while literature is fixed in print. Folklore is often composed and transmitted anonymously, while most literature has an author. Folklore is informally transmitted, non-institutional culture, while literature is backed by (institutional) publishing houses, and in its print life often becomes canonical and thus institutional. Folklore is frequently performed in face-to-face modes, while literature can be consumed privately. We look for variation in folklore, expecting to see different versions of jokes and fairy tales and holiday customs, while literature once composed and published tends to stay the same.

Of course these boundaries can be somewhat permeable, which is one reason it's fruitful to discuss folklore and literature together. The crossroads where folklore and literature meet is, from our disciplinary perspective, called folklore in literature, and that's what this chapter is about.

First – both topically and chronologically – it's important to acknowledge that much literature comes from folklore; in fact, folklore can be considered the literature of earlier time periods, whether pre-literate or non-literate or whatever. Narrative folklore such as folktales, myths, and legends *were* the long-form entertainment of their day, communally told rather than privately consumed in novel or comic book form. I'm not interested in a debate about origins, and I'm not trying to draw a harsh dividing line between pre-literate and literate societies; mostly, I'm trying to point out that folklore has fulfilled many of the same functions that literature does.

It's also significant that folklore and literature have much in common. Both involve artistic uses of language; both can bridge fiction and fact: recall that some folk narrative genres, like folktale and fairy tale, are deemed fictional, as with literary genres like the novel; other folk narrative genres, like myth and legend, are told as true, and similarly we have literary genres like memoir and biography that are supposed to be grounded in truth. Both fiction and fact utilize artistic devices such as misdirection and inversion, and both draw on intertextual strategies to make sense and make meaning (discussed in de Caro and Jordan, 3-4).

Next, we can talk about why and how folklore appears in literature. Alan Dundes pioneered this approach with his 1965 publication, "The Study of Folklore in Literature and Culture: Identification and Interpretation." In it, Dundes urges scholars to first identify the folklore being employed in literature, and then interpret how it is used. He writes: "Naive analyses can result from inadequate or inaccurate identification. Plots of traditional tale types might be falsely attributed to individual writers; European themes in a European tale told by American Indians might be mistakenly considered to be aboriginal elements" (136).

In other words, you'll look like an idiot if you assume that a given element in a literary work is uniquely the author's creation, rather than being an item from folklore that the author chose to incorporate. Not recognizing how heavily Chaucer (or Shakespeare, or… take your pick of famous authors, really) borrowed from folktales in *The Canterbury Tales* is just silly, for instance.

Folklorists Frank de Caro and Rosan A. Jordan suggest that a third step beyond identification and interpretation is necessary. They want to get at the *why* of it:

> *[W]hy* is there so much folklore in literature? Why have writers felt this urge to re-situate folkloric communication in the literary? Obviously, it is partly a matter of the realistic reflection of sociocultural realities…insofar as, say, literary fictional narratives (or, for that matter, visual arts texts) mirror the real world and insofar as folkloric communication is part of that world, folklore inevitably appears in the literary text. (14)

Thus, because art imitates life in various ways, literary art must at least make a nod to folklore since folklore is a fact of human social life. But de Caro and Jordan also point out that writers can in theory draw from tons of material: "Why does (s)he choose in some instances folklore, as opposed to (or, for that matter, in conjunction with) pop cultural media, culturally determined kinship systems, or aspects of utilitarian technology" (14)? What makes folklore special?

In trying to answer these questions, folklorists working at the intersections of folklore and literature are digging deep into the meanings that different realms of culture connote, themselves a form of folklore (worldview or folk idea, perhaps; the ideas people hold about assigning value are always of interest to cultural scholars). This sort of work is also an assertion that even in the digital age, in a time of ephemeral connection like that epitomized by Snapchat, folklore is still a meaningful bond connecting people, so meaningful that it worms its way into literature, whether or not we realize it as authors, readers, or publishers.

Another reason this is a thriving area of folklore research is because it's not like we're going to run out of analytical fodder. In 2016, I gave a paper at the annual meeting of the American Folklore Society that would exemplify this approach, applying it to *The Fall of the Kings by* Ellen Kushner and Delia Sherman,[1] for example. And a lot of fairy-tale scholarship also studies the uses of fairy tales in other forms of culture, from literature to film to fanfic.

So, if you're going to go this route, remember to identify the folklore in its literary context; interpret it (how is it changed now that it's in print?); and then ask *why* it's been utilized in this fashion. What can folklore accomplish that nothing else can? The starting place is, a lot!

References:

De Caro, Frank, and Rosan Augusta Jordan. *Re-Situating Folk-*

lore: Folk Contexts and Twentieth-Century Literature and Art. The University of Tennessee Press, 2004.

Dundes, Alan. "The Study of Folklore in Literature and Culture: Identification and Interpretation." *Journal of American Folklore* vol. 78, no. 308, 1965, pp. 136-142.

MYTH-RITUAL THEORY

IF YOU THINK myth is a popular topic for scholars of all stripes to sink their teeth into, just wait til you see what happens when we throw ritual into the mix!

Myth-ritual theory seeks to understand the intersections of myth and ritual. It is unique in asserting that there is a connection at all, because typically the scholars drawn to myth have studied it from religious or literary perspectives, while the scholars drawn to ritual have tried to understand ritual from anthropological or religious perspectives. To unite myth and ritual as cultural components of meaning-making asserts that they fulfill similar, if not interdependent, functions in a society.

This theoretical approach originated in the nineteenth century and hasn't been popular for a while, but I still think it offers an important paradigm for what folklore studies used to look like. Alan Dundes characterizes myth-ritual theory as such:

> As myth texts were assumed to represent reflections from ritual, the nineteenth-century preoccupation with searching for origins centered on reconstructing the supposed rituals which had given rise to the myths. Most commonly the initiating ritual was said to be a calendrical or seasonal one. So as the death of winter yielded to the birth or rebirth of spring in predictable cyclical fashion, so there were myths of renewal like the cleansing effect of a primeval deluge in which an older world was destroyed and a new one created. (110)

Dundes also points out that, for all that it's tough to prove early connections between myth and ritual, the theory had a beneficial effect on the study of myth: it encouraged literary scholars to take into account cultural context and not just focus on the myth texts themselves.

William Robertson Smith, a Biblical and Arabic scholar, pioneered this concept in the late 1880s. He asserted that myth derived from ritual in ancient Greece and beyond. This, however, designated a hierarchy between myth and ritual. As myth scholar Robert Segal points out: "Myth was superfluous as long as the reason for the ritual remained clear. Only once the reason was lost was myth created to explain and perhaps to justify the ritual, which might nevertheless have continued to be practiced anyway" (2).

Other major scholars to work with myth-ritual theory include James Frazer (known for articulating the concept of sympathetic magic) and anthropologists Clyde Kluckhohn and (to a degree) Claude Lévi-Strauss, as well as other scholars working on classics, literature, and culture. Kluckhohn and others believed that when myths and rituals are found together, they fulfill separate functions (the myth explains what the ritual enacts). Kluckhohn also argued that myth and ritual both serve the psychological function of alleviating anxiety by providing prescribed ways of understanding (as with myth) and prescribed ways of behaving (as with ritual; summarized in Segal 10-12).

There are valid reasons to ask whether myth-ritual theory can give us the whole picture, though. For one thing, its execution has been a bit ethnocentric, with a lot of focus on ancient and supposedly-primitive cultures (Joseph Fontenrose has published a big take-down of Frazer's assertion that the myth-ritual connection is all about king-killing; see Segal 436-443). For another, early myth-ritual scholars have tended to ignore the gendered implications of their assertions (but this is my standard feminist critique of older scholarship). From what I gather, classicist Jane Harrison did attempt to account for the role of the feminine divine in her adaptations of myth-ritual theory, but there hasn't been a ton of feminist critique of myth-ritual scholarship, at least not that I've found.

Still, you can't talk about myth, ritual, and religion without talking about myth-ritual theory, no matter what your disciplinary perspective is. As Segal concludes:

> Whatever the actual nexus between myths and rituals turns out to be, the myth-ritualist theory remains valuable. It suggests aspects of myth that might otherwise get overlooked – notably, the relationship between belief and practice, between narrative and action. The theory also suggests parallels between myth

> and other cultural phenomena like science and literature
> that might otherwise get missed. (13)

Thinking about culture, religion, and narrative with myth-ritual theory as a framing concept is bound to yield some insights, even if some of the premises contained therein are worth interrogating.

References:

Dundes, Alan, editor. *Sacred Narrative: Readings in the Theory of Myth.* University of California Press, 1984.

Segal, Robert A., editor. *The Myth and Ritual Theory.* Blackwell Publishers Inc., 1998.

UNILINEAR EVOLUTION

AN IMPORTANT CHAPTER in the discipline's history is sadly very racist, but that makes it all the more important to learn about.

In my 2016 keynote on the body in folklore,[1] I talked about how early folklore scholarship either completely ignored the body, or made awful, ethnocentric generalizations about non-Western bodies (especially "primitive" bodies). In order to understand this part of our disciplinary history, it helps to know what unilinear evolution is.

Unilinear evolution is a nineteenth-century scholarly paradigm hypothesizing that all human societies passed through the same stages of civilization (or lack thereof) in the same order: savagery, barbarism, and finally civilization. Societies climbed up these phases like rungs on a ladder, and what's more, since the ladder itself was thought to be universal, groups occupying the same rung could be usefully compared to one another, whether they're contemporaneous or not.

British anthropologist Edward B. Tylor was a major proponent of this view, but there were others as well. Notably for folklorists, Sir James George Frazer (who gave us the concept of sympathetic magic) adhered to this view.

As Alan Dundes points out, Frazer's belief in unilinear evolution led to shoddy scholarly practices and imprecise conclusions:

> To illuminate folklore (which was essentially limited to the traditions of peasants living in a state of barbarism of the vestiges thereof retained among civilized peoples), it was necessary to compare folklore items with what Frazer assumed were the fuller, more complete, and "original" forms still to be found among contemporary "savages." With this premise and its assumption of universalism, Frazer felt perfectly justified in taking data out of particular cultural contexts to be cited in his vast compendiums of "parallels" to particular myths and customs. (*International Folkloristics* 110)

Andrew Lang, known for his "Colored Fairy" books as well as his anthropology scholarship, is another figure who crosses into the history of folkloristics and subscribed to unilinear evolution. He wrote:

> The student of folklore is thus led to examine the usages, myths and ideas of savages, which are all still retained in rude enough shape, by the European peasantry...In proverbs and riddles, and nursery tales and

> superstitions, we detect the relics of a stage of thought, which is dying out in Europe, but which still exists in many parts of the world. (quoted in Dundes, *Folklore Matters* 58-59)

This is, obviously, a problematic take on things. As Dundes points out:

> The apparent irrationality of folklore could be explained by understanding such folklore in the light of primitive thought where it was intelligible...According to this somewhat racist, ethnocentric theory, primitive people were incapable of thinking in terms of causal logic, a view echoed in the mid-twentieth century by C. G. Jung. (59)

Ah, Dundes could never resist a dig at Jung, or Campbell for that matter. And people wonder where I got my hyper-critical approach to Campbell's work!

Anyway, the last century's scholars weren't all sold on unilinear evolution. I like this snippet from Franz Boas, another founding father of American anthropology who was also involved in folklore studies:

> It must, therefore, be clearly understood that anthropological research which compares similar cultural phenomena from various parts of the world, in order to discover the uniform history of their

> development, makes the assumption that the same ethnological phenomenon has everywhere developed in the same manner. Here lies the flaw in the argument of the new method, for no such proof can be given. Even the most cursory review shows that the same phenomena may develop in a multitude of ways. (quoted in Dundes, *Folklore Matters* 59).

Sadly, however, this rhetoric has been embalmed in our discipline's history. For example, the concept of the "folk" used to be very ethnocentric, though the way we use "folk group" now is much more expansive.

When teaching introduction to folklore at UC Berkeley in spring 2017, I introduced the concept of unilinear evolution early in the class, like in the third week, when covering myth. Additionally, myth-ritual theory (covered in the previous chapter) is steeped in assumptions about the evolutionary relationships between not only myth and ritual but the "stages" of humanity. But unilinear evolution also influences the study of customary folklore (particularly folk belief and folk medicine) as well as children's folklore, and so I mentioned the concept during those units of my class as well.

Understanding unilinear evolution is crucial to understanding the development of anthropology and folkloristics, as well as some of the terms and theories that are still in circulation today. It's helpful to examine our own biases, as scholars and more generally as cultural beings, and I think knowing this disciplinary history helps us do better to avoid ethnocentrism.

References:

Dundes, Alan. *Folklore Matters*. The University of Tennessee Press, 1989.

---, editor. *International Folkloristics: Classic Contributions by the Founders of Folklore*. Rowman & Littlefield Publishers Inc., 1999.

HORIZONTAL VS. VERTICAL TRANSMISSION

In folklore studies we like to nerd out about how precisely folklore gets transmitted, in large part because how folklore is transmitted is a key way of distinguishing it from other types of culture. That's where this handy distinction comes in.

Puzzling through how folklore is transmitted, and what makes this transmission different than other modes of culture (pop culture; the mass media; literature) is one of the key questions we address in my discipline. Understanding how folklore gets transmitted between adjacent groups is an important part of the puzzle piece, and that's why I like to teach my students about horizontal vs. vertical transmission.

We know that folk groups are not homogeneous or monolithic; the different members might be invested in that identity at different levels or in varying ways. Knowing someone's religion or ethnicity or career doesn't let you make a ton of assumptions about their identity without also knowing their gender, nationality, sexual orientation, and more.

When describing how transmission happens within folk

groups, we refer to active vs. passive bearers, or those who can competently perform a folklore text vs. those who recognize it but don't necessarily transmit it.

But when we want to talk about how folklore is used to uphold group boundaries, or what happens when folklore is transmitted between groups separated by hierarchies, I like to use the concept of horizontal vs. vertical transmission.

In horizontal transmission, folklore is transmitted between members of a folk group that do not have major hierarchies separating them, such as age, social class, or other authoritative titles (being a religious leader or head of family, for example). In vertical transmission, folklore is transmitted across those hierarchies, either from a higher-up member of a folk group to a lower-down one, or from a folk group that is hierarchically ranked above another adjacent group to members of that lower-down group.

My favorite example is how in children's folklore, folklore transmitted from one child to another would be considered horizontal transmission, while folklore transmitted from adult to child (like a lullaby) would be considered vertical transmission. Age – and legal adult status – definitely count as a hierarchy in my view.

Other examples of how to use these terms might come from folk groups that cohere around the practice of folk religion, with higher-ranking members vertically transmitting lore to lower-ranking members, or members of equal status transmitting lore horizontally to one another. In occupational folk groups, too, we find people who don't necessarily occupy institutionally powerful roles (because, again, that's not as interesting to folklorists), but rather are recognized within their peer groups as more experienced hence deserving of respect. These old-timers would transmit lore vertically to the newcomers, while people on more equal footing would transmit lore to one another horizontally.

The idea of relating the transmission of folklore to social power is not a new one. As I write in a blog post on folklore and power:[1]

> One of the seminal works addressing the relationship of identity and power in folklore is Richard Bauman's "Differential Identity and the Social Base of Folklore." Bauman's examples, drawn from genres such as taunts and jokes that bridge the communicative spaces between social groups, demonstrate that folklore is a response to and is inextricably wrapped up in the relationships among groups of people with differing access to control over their circumstances (Bauman 1972). Bauman's essay initiated a shift in folkloristics towards performance as an orienting model. Rather than focusing on the folklore text, scholars began studying the context in which the text was situated, some going so far as to claim that there *is* no originary [sic] text, but instead that folklore is emergent, created in performance (Bauman 1984).

The shift toward performance helped illuminate many of the ways in which power structures folklore events. Patricia Sawin is one of Bauman's students and one of the few folklorists to apply the power-oriented gender and identity theories of Judith Butler to performance theories of folklore, arguing that comprehensive studies of folklore and power must begin "by looking for evidence of a power imbalance and ask how the esthetic event impinges on and plays out for the less powerful participants" (Sawin, 55). In her work with traditional singer Bessie Eldreth, Sawin demonstrates that "esthetic performance is a central arena in which gender identities and differential social power based on gender are engaged" (48). In other words, folklore performances – which range from song-singing and story-telling sessions to kinesthetic events such as folk-dances and festivals to the creation and consumption of material culture like holiday foods or customary garments – are fraught with power. Power can be contested or reinforced within a performance, and the power at stake need not be gender relations, but could also be ethnic or national tensions.

Describing the transmission of folklore in relation to hierarchy applies no matter what big category of folklore we're talking about: verbal, customary, or material. That's because folklore occurs in many a medium, and it's not the medium through which it's expressed that makes it folklore, but rather the mode of transmission.

This insight – that its transmission is what makes folklore unique – is why Lynne McNeill writes: "Well, you try to explain what a creation myth, a jump-rope rhyme, a Fourth of July BBQ, and some bathroom graffiti have in common, and you'll find it's not a terribly easy task" (2).

Attention to the transmission of folklore thus lets us study seemingly disparate topics under the aegis of one discipline. And, as I argue in this chapter, awareness of social hierarchies plays a key role in how (well) we do this.

I should note that my use of these terms is not universal. My colleague William Pooley, critiquing the phylogenetic analysis that's recently come up (and not been well-received by folklorists), notes:

> The authors say that they found that many tales are surprisingly limited to vertical rather than horizontal transmission, by which they mean that – contrary to what we might expect – tales tend to travel down through the generations within cultural or linguistic groups, rather than between groups who live next to one another.[2]

So in this sense, horizontal and vertical connote whether folklore is transmitted through time in a space-bound group, or throughout space among contemporaneous groups. This use goes back to at least Elias Lönnrot, author of the Finnish national epic *The Kalevala.* In folklorist Lauri Honko's interpretation of Lönnrot's research (that has superorganic and possibly devolutionary assumptions going on, addressed in the next chapter), he writes: "Lönnrot regarded the vertical transmission of tradition from one generation to the next as more conservative and preservative than the horizontal spreading of a song often after a single hearing."[3]

I instead use the terms synchronic and diachronic to refer to these phenomena as we study them, where synchronic means something happening at the same time and diachronic means something happening over time. The main idea holds, though: it's useful to know how much folklore is persisting over time and who is transmitting it, though I like the fact that the contemporary use of vertical vs. horizontal transmission emphasizes identity and hierarchy since obviously those are really important facets of culture too.

Anyway, if you're in one of my folklore classes, you'll undoubtedly get introduced to these terms. What are some other examples of horizontal vs. vertical folklore transmission that come to mind?

References:

Bauman, Richard. "Differential Identity and the Social Base of Folklore." *Toward New Perspectives in Folklore,* edited by. Américo Paredes and Richard Bauman, University of Texas Press, 1972, 31-41.

Bauman, Richard. *Verbal Art as Performance*. Waveland Press, Inc., 1984 [1977].

McNeill, Lynne S. *Folklore Rules: A Fun, Quick, and Useful Introduction to the Field of Academic Folklore Studies*. Utah State University Press, 2013.

Sawin, Patricia. "Performance at the Nexus of Gender, Power, and Desire: Reconsidering Bauman's Verbal Art as Performance from the Perspective of Gendered Subjectivity as Performance." *Journal of American Folklore* vol. 115, no. 455, 2002, pp. 28-61.

THE DEVOLUTIONARY PREMISE

WHERE DOES FOLKLORE COME FROM? And where does it go? The devolutionary premise represents one attempt to answer these questions, but it's pretty biased.

While folklorists today aren't all that concerned with origins, that's not true of our past. And by "past" I mean like the nineteenth century. We used to rigorously debate how, when, where, and why folklore originated, and we had theories to help explain it. Put briefly, folklore is NOT just fossilized (elite) culture.

The concept of unilinear evolution, or the notion that every society ascends the same ladder of the stages of civilization, is one I addressed in the previous chapter. It's not pretty. Similarly hierarchical and problematic is the devolutionary premise of folklore.

As in many arenas, Alan Dundes has done pioneering work here. He wrote: "The most common devolutionary notion is that folklore decays through time. Another notion is that folklore 'runs down' by moving from 'higher' to 'lower' strata of society" (6).

Among other examples, we see this in the theory of *gesunkenes Kulturgut* (which translates to "sunken culture"), promoted by Hans Naumann, which claimed that social elites were the creators of expressive culture, which from there filtered down to lower strata (usually in a corrupted or polluted form). The Grimms believed that many folktales were incomplete, corrupted myth texts. Additionally, the widely held idea that the "original" version of a text is the fullest and most complete version has tinges of devolutionary premise to it.

Related to another topic I've covered earlier in this book, Dundes points out that the devolutionary premise is evident in Axel Olrik's epic laws of folk narrative, writing: "Even Olrik's so-called epic laws of folklore were presumed to weaken in time. Olrik suggested, for example, that the law of the number three 'gradually succumbs to intellectual demands for greater realism'" (10).

Similarly, the myth-ritual theory is one expression of the devolutionary premise, and its hold on people's imaginations remains quite strong. I see it appearing in literature, such as in *The Fall of the Kings* by Ellen Kushner and Delia Sherman.

Dundes mentions E. B. Tylor as another early scholar who promoted the devolutionary premise, though not always explicitly, writing:

> The association of folklore with the past, glorious or not, continued. Progress meant leaving the past behind. From this perspective, the noble savage and the equally noble peasant – folkloristically speaking – were destined to

> lose their folklore as they marched ineffably toward civilization. Thus it was not a matter of the evolution *of* folklore; it was more a matter of the evolution *out of* folklore. This may best be seen in the work of Tylor who in adamantly opposing rigid degenerative theories definitely championed unilinear cultural evolution. (12)

This idea is still alive and kicking. If you've heard of cultures evolving beyond certain outdated or even "primitive" beliefs, you've encountered the evolutionary take on the devolutionary premise. And this has serious implications for our discipline, because if folklore's always dying out, will we as folklorists have jobs a few decades from now?

I'm fortunate to have studied under Dundes, because as he constantly reminded his students, we are all part of the folk, and hence we all have folklore. Once you move the definition of "folk" away from antiquated peasant or rural group identities, you arrive at a more expansive definition of folklore that is constantly developing and updating. This is similar to the premise of salvage anthropology, prominent in 19th and early-to-mid 20th versions of the discipline: the "oh no, traditional cultures are disappearing, gotta document and save 'em while you can" rhetoric that was popular for longer than it should have been. Yes, culture is always changing, but it's the height of hubris to assume that we scholars happen to be the ones to stumble upon the purest, most authentic version of a culture just in time to save it!

So, no, folklorists won't be out of a job anytime soon, despite the prevalence of the devolutionary premise. In fact, it's in all of our best interests to combat it, not just to keep folklorists working but also to assert a more accurate view of culture that's not strictly hierarchical.

References:

Dundes, Alan. "The Devolutionary Premise in Folklore Theory." *Journal of the Folklore Institute* vol. 6, no. 1, 1969, pp. 5-19.

CONCLUSION: HAVING LEARNED ABOUT FOLKLORE, NOW WHAT?

WELL, now that you've read some, most, or all of this book, you may be wondering… what now? What do I do with all this folklore knowledge inside my brain?! (I ask myself that on a daily basis, which is one of the reasons this book now exists!) I have a couple suggestions, plus I'm making what scholars call a claim for significance - in other words, why you should care about this - but I'm addressing people in the real world, not so much my fellow academic folklorists.

When people learn that I'm a folklorist, their response is often some version of, "Oh, how cool!" Folklore is a topic that touches everyone's lives, and it's a fun one, too. I wrote this book so that everyone who wanted to take a folklore class but didn't get a chance to in college would be able to take a quick dive into the field of academic folklore studies. Maybe not every single chapter resonates with you, but hopefully you found something that spoke to you and your interests. I also wrote this book in case colleagues want to assign it to students, and in case my friends and family who I don't see nearly often enough because I'm a bit of a workaholic can get some more insight into what I spend most of my time doing. I wouldn't necessarily say this book is my love letter to folklore studies, but hopefully it conveys all my enthusiasm around having amassed so much really cool knowledge and my excitement at sharing it.

Beyond providing information that isn't always accessible to the general public, one of my major goals has been to inspire readers to get more curious about the folklore in their own lives. I'd love for y'all to take what you learned in this book and see where it manifests in your own social lives and relationships. Maybe there's family folklore you can document, or maybe there's folklore in your workplace or hobby group that you can look at with more understanding. Maybe you're a writer looking to use folklore in your work, which I think is awesome because I do it too! There are SO many ways that folklore weaves in and out of our lives, so I'm just happy when someone learns about folklore and starts to see these connections on their own.

For some, the next logical step is to study more folklore on your own time. Please raid the references I've included in many chapters, or hit me up on Twitter for book recommendations (I'm @foxyfolklorist). Talk to your local librarian for suggestions. A few people may want to take other folklore classes; as of now, some of the most accessible online classes are offered by my colleagues Brittany Warman and Sara Cleto at The Carterhaugh School of Folklore and the Fantastic[1] (like me, they tend to be very narrative-focused, plus they do a lot of folklore and literature connections). If you want to specifically know more about the links between folklore and fiction, you can look up Ceallaigh S. MacCath-Moran's Folklore and Fiction website.[2] The team at Folkwise[3] does live streams every week of folklore-related video games while interviewing folklore experts. There are a handful of folklore podcasts out there, too. If you're considering a Master's degree or doctorate in folklore, again, feel free to reach out to inquire about which schools are offering degrees, or you could be proactive and count on Indiana University being one of them and going to their website to look for resources. The American Folklore Society also has a list of current folklore programs on their website.

Anyway, I'm all for further official folklore studies, but non-academics can also stay reasonably informed about the field. I dislike the kinds of gatekeeping that often happen in university systems, so for me it's less about "you have to have a fancy, expensive degree to contribute to our conferences, publications, etc." than "you should be respectful enough to educate yourself about the basics of the field before you come play in our sandbox." Like, maybe you should read enough of our scholarship to understand why it's maybe not a great idea to come in touting Joseph Campbell's hero's journey as the end-all and be-all of narrative theory, perhaps? I know my tone is often snarky and irreverent, and I'm all for the texts that serve as gateway drugs to the delightful body of work we have going on, but trust me, there is *so much* more to folklore studies than what you see on the shelves at Barnes & Noble or in the "folklore and mythology" section of Kindle books on Amazon. Illustrating the longevity and depth of folklore studies has been one of my major goals in this book, whether or not you're all in to pursue graduate work in it.

Remember: we're all the folk. We all have lore. We all participate in this informal, highly democratic, delightfully artistic form of culture. Now, go forth and engage with folklore!

END NOTES

Text, Texture, and Context

1. Jorgensen, Jeana. "Hello Blog! Let's Talk about Fairy Tales!" *Patheos*, 19 October 2011, https://www.patheos.com/blogs/foxyfolklorist/hello-blog-lets-talk-about-fairy-tales/

Fieldwork

1. "Fieldwork Guides." *Traditional Arts Indiana*, https://traditionalarts.indiana.edu/Resources/Fieldwork%20Guides.html. Accessed 15 October 2021.
2. "Folklore's Four Sisters: Scholarship, Fieldwork, Activism, and Artistry." *CityLore*, July 2021, https://citylore.org/2021/07/folklores-four-sisters/. Accessed 15 October 2021.
3. *The American Folklife Center*. https://www.loc.gov/folklife/ Accessed 15 October 2021.

Worldview

1. Jorgensen, Jeana. "#FolkloreThursday: The Culture Reflector Theory." *Patheos*, 19 May 2016, https://www.patheos.com/blogs/foxyfolklorist/folklorethursday-the-culture-reflector-theory/
2. Jorgensen, Jeana. "The Body in Folklore Keynote: Introduction." *Patheos*, 13 May 2016, https://www.patheos.com/blogs/foxyfolklorist/the-body-in-folklore-keynote-introduction/

Folk Group

1. Jorgensen, Jeana. "#FolkloreThursday: Where Does the Term 'Folklore' Come From?" *Patheos*, 16 June 2016, https://www.patheos.com/blogs/foxyfolklorist/folklorethursday-where-does-the-term-folklore-come-from/

Motif vs. Theme

1. I know I could spend hours on their website; check it out! http://tvtropes.org/
2. Jorgensen, Jeana. "The Body in Folklore Keynote: Folk Narrative." *Patheos,* 13 May 2016, https://www.patheos.com/blogs/foxyfolklorist/the-body-in-folklore-keynote-folk-narrative/
3. One university site that catalogues the *Motif Index*: http://www.ruthenia.ru/folklore/thompson/. The other site: https://sites.ualberta.ca/~urban/Projects/English/Motif_Index.htm

Tale Type

1. Kinnes, Tormod. "The AT Divisions of Tales." http://oaks.nvg.org/folktale-types.html#atu
2. Kinnes, Tormod. "The ATU System." http://oaks.nvg.org/uther.html

The Epic Laws of Folk Narrative

1. Jorgensen, Jeana. "#ICFA38: Fantastic Epics (Conference Recap." *Patheos,* 4 April 2017, https://www.patheos.com/blogs/foxyfolklorist/icfa-38-fantastic-epics-conference-recap/

Joke Cycle

1. Jorgensen, Jeana. "Dehumanized and Rationalized." *Patheos,* 25 November 2016, https://www.patheos.com/blogs/foxyfolklorist/dehumanized-and-rationalized-16/

Myth

1. "How the Moon and Stars Came to Be." *Creation Myths from the Philippines,* 2003, https://sites.pitt.edu/~dash/creation-phil.html#howthemoon
2. "The Will-o'-the-Wisp." *Will-o'-the-wisp; Jack-o'-Lantern,* 2021, https://sites.pitt.edu/~dash/willowisp.html#goodrich

Legend

1. *The Origin of Underground People,* 2012, https://sites.pitt.edu/~dash/originunder.html

Folktale

1. Folklorist D.L. Ashliman has assembled many Runaway Pancake texts on his site: https://sites.pitt.edu/~dash/type2025.html
2. Jorgensen, Jeana. "Fairy Tales and #TwitterTypes." *Patheos,* 10 January 2012, https://www.patheos.com/blogs/foxyfolklorist/fairy-tales-and-twittertypes/

Fairy Tale

1. Heiner, Heidi Anne. "Earliest Fairy Tales." *SurLaLune Fairytales.com.* https://www.surlalunefairytales.com/intro-pages/earliest-fairy-tales.html

Ballad

1. Winick, Stephen. "From *Wit and Mirth* to *Secret Songs of Silence*: A Brief Introduction to Bawdy Songs." *Huffpost,* 28 January 2013, https://www.huffpost.com/entry/bawdy-songs_b_2548294
2. *The Max Hunter Folk Song Collection.* https://maxhunter.missouristate.edu/
3. *English Broadside Ballad Archive.* http://ebba.english.ucsb.edu/
4. "Pearl Bryan." *Criminal,* 6 August 2015, https://thisiscriminal.com/episode-24-pearl-bryan-8-7-2015/
5. "The Portrait," *Criminal,* 27 August 2015, https://thisiscriminal.com/episode-25-the-portrait/
6. These links are cogently explained in Amelia Mason's "The Hidden Roots of 'Hunger Games' Hit Song? Murder Ballads, Civil Rights Hymns," *WBUR News,* 10 December 2014, https://www.wbur.org/news/2014/12/10/hunger-games-mockingjay
7. *Broadside Ballads Online from the Bodleian Libraries.* http://ballads.bodleian.ox.ac.uk/

8. Waltz, Robert B., editor. *The Traditional Ballad Index*. 2021. http://www.csufresno.edu/folklore/BalladIndexTOC.html

Folk Music & Folk Song

1. "Folk Music and Song," *American Folklife Center,* 30 January 2013, https://www.loc.gov/folklife/guide/folkmusicandsong.html
2. "Folk Music." *The American Folklife Center* blog. https://blogs.loc.gov/folklife/category/folk-music/
3. "Lomax Family at the American Folklife Center," *The American Folklife Center,* 12 February 2016, https://www.loc.gov/folklife/lomax/lomaxcentennial.html?loclr=blogflt

Folk Dance

1. Houston, Ron. "What is Folk Dance?" *The Society of Folk Dance Historians,* 2018, https://sfdh.us/encyclopedia/what_is_folk_dance_houston.html
2. Jorgensen, Jeana. "The Body in Folklore Keynote: Body Art & Dance." *Patheos,* 14 May 2016, https://www.patheos.com/blogs/foxyfolklorist/the-body-in-folklore-keynote-body-art-dance/

Folk Medicine

1. From the book's publication page at Utah State University Press: https://digitalcommons.usu.edu/usupress_pubs/64/

Body Art

1. Jorgensen, Jeana. "The Self is the First Audience." *Patheos,* 29 September 2014, https://www.patheos.com/blogs/foxyfolklorist/the-self-is-the-first-audience/

Occupational Folklore

1. New York Folklore. https://nyfolklore.org/

Family Folklore

1. Jorgensen, Jeana. "Emotional Labor and Gender." *Patheos,* 10 September 2016, https://www.patheos.com/blogs/foxyfolklorist/emotional-labor-and-gender/
2. Jorgensen, Jeana. "Kin-Keeping and Worry-Work." *Patheos,* 11 September 2016, https://www.patheos.com/blogs/foxyfolklorist/kin-keeping-and-worry-work/

Folklore and Disability

1. Jorgensen, Jeana. "A Rant on Helen Oyeyemi's Boy, Snow, Bird." *Patheos,* 29 May 2019, https://www.patheos.com/blogs/foxyfolklorist/a-rant-on-helen-oyeyemis-boy-snow-bird/
2. Cleto, Sara. "Disability in Netflix's The Dragon Prince." *Through the Twisted Woods,* 23 September 2018, https://throughthetwistedwoods.wordpress.com/2018/09/23/disability-in-netflixs-the-dragon-prince/

Folklore In/And Literature

1. Jorgensen, Jeana. "My 2016 AFS Proposal on Myth-Ritual Theory in The Fall of the Kings." *Patheos,* 14 October 2016, https://www.patheos.com/blogs/foxyfolklorist/my-2016-afs-proposal-on-myth-ritual-theory-in-the-fall-of-the-kings/

Unilinear Evolution

1. Jorgensen, Jeana. "The Body in Folklore Keynote: Folklore Scholarship & Theory." *Patheos,* 13 May 2016, https://www.patheos.com/blogs/foxyfolklorist/the-body-in-folklore-keynote-folklore-scholarship-theory/

Horizontal vs. Vertical Transmission

1. Jorgensen, Jeana. "Essay on Folklore and Power." *Patheos,* 27 June 2012, https://www.patheos.com/blogs/foxyfolklorist/essay-on-folklore-and-power/
2. Pooley, William. "Fairytale Genetics." *Will Pooley,* 22 January 2016,

https://williamgpooley.wordpress.com/2016/01/22/fairytale-genetics/
3. Honko, Lauri. "The Five Performances of the Kalevala," *The Folklore Fellows Network* 29 June 2009 [2003], https://www.folklorefellows.fi/the-five-performances-of-the-kalevala/

Conclusion: Having Learned About Folklore, Now What?

1. *The Carterhaugh School of Folklore and the Fantastic.* https://carterhaughschool.com/
2. *Folklore and Fiction; Ceallaigh S. MacCath-Moran.* http://folkloreandfiction.com/
3. *Folkwise Linktree.* https://linktr.ee/Folkwise

INDEX

ACKNOWLEDGMENTS

First, I must thank Lynne S. McNeill and the Utah State University Press for so graciously allowing me to quote extended portions of *Folklore Rules*. That book does, in fact, rule...so please consider picking up a copy if you haven't already! It deserves all the hype!

My cover designer, Cover Villain, and my editor, Donna Martz, have both done stellar jobs in helping my book find its way into the world.

Gigantic thanks go to my writer friends who encouraged me to undertake this project, and who supported me throughout, especially: Jen Stevenson who held my hand in early stages, Kess Eldridge who invited me to her wise and snarky writer's group, and all the people in said writer's group (unlisted here because either there are too many to name, or they prefer the cover of anonymity so no one knows what giant nerds they are, you decide).

The folklore community has also been incredibly supportive. Special thanks go to the colleagues who provided early reviews of my book that I could use as promotional material: Libby Tucker, Patricia Sawin, Susan Redington Bobby, Sara Cleto, and Psyche Ready. The Folkwise crew has been encouraging throughout and has provided many a laugh during this process (thank you for Meme Mondays!). Even colleagues I don't see regularly have gone out of their way to express enthusiasm for this project, which means a lot to me since I often feel like I'm on the margins of the discipline due to not landing a tenure-track professorship.

My friends and larger communities have also played a role in making this book happen. My dance troupe and dance students were unflaggingly encouraging, and were quite kind and accommodating when my brain was still in writing mode when I showed up to teach dance. The readers of my Patheos blog, where I initially composed many of the posts that would become chapters in this book, were a fantastic first audience. My folklore buddy Linda and my favorite human Ryan have both been awesome throughout, as well as my sister Sam, who got a mention in the Dedication but is so great she deserves another shout-out.

ABOUT THE AUTHOR

Dr. Jeana Jorgensen studied folklore at the University of California, Berkeley under Alan Dundes and went on to earn a PhD in folklore from Indiana University. She has authored over 25 academic articles and book chapters in addition to blog posts, poems, stories, and rants. She spends entirely too much time on Twitter (@foxyfolklorist), dances, and plays with her sourdough starter.

To learn more about her upcoming books and sign up for her newsletter, you can go to: www.folklore101.com

Printed in Great Britain
by Amazon

24417057R00199